North
Ghost Lig

T012836?

North Carolina
GHOST LIGHTS
AND
LEGENDS

CHARLES F. GRITZNER

ϟϟϟ

Blair is an imprint of Carolina Wren Press.

The mission of Blair/Carolina Wren Press is to seek out, nurture,
and promote literary work by new and underrepresented writers.

We gratefully acknowledge the ongoing support of general
operations by the Durham Arts Council's United Arts Fund.

Library of Congress Control Number: 2019930754

In memory of John B. Rehder, PhD,
who introduced me to North's Carolina
ghost lights and legends and thereby opened
the door to my more than half-century fascination
with the phenomena and provided the
inspiration for this book

⚡ ⚡ ⚡

Contents

CHAPTER THREE

East Central 53

CHAPTER FOUR

Southeast 79

CHAPTER SEVEN

Reflections 163

Preface

Strange happenings—many of which fall within the realm of so-called paranormal or supernatural—have long fascinated me. As a high school student in the early 1950s, I became an avid reader of Frank Edward's books on weird phenomena. His accounts provided the early nurturing of an interest in peculiar anomalies that continues today.

As a professional geographer who taught at the college level for fifty years, my research interests were wide ranging and spanned a considerable array of topics. Among the seventy-some different courses I taught during my career, most were traditional geographical subjects, whereas several clearly bordered the margins of traditional geographical inquiry. Among the latter were courses developed and taught on the "Geography of Conflict," "Geography of the Future" (few true or false answers there!), "Geomythography," and "Geography of the Paranormal." To my knowledge, the courses in geographic myths (which also touched on a small number of paranormal phenomena) and "Geography of the Paranormal" were unique in American geography.

Many readers, no doubt, associate geography with the dull memorization of states, capitals, highest mountains, longest rivers, and major products. In this context it is important to understand the nature of the science: geography is not based on the study of any particular set of earthbound phenomena. Rather, like history (time), geography is a methodology (space), one that can be applied to anything and everything appearing on Earth's surface. A subject such as ghost lights and their associated legends admittedly is marginal to the primary focus of geographical inquiry and analysis. In fact, very few academicians in any discipline have studied such features. That said, there is absolutely no rational reason such subjects cannot, or should not, be studied by scientists. After all, they exist in one form or another, either as actual features or happenings or as deep-seated beliefs held by individuals or within a particular cultural system.

Sadly, far too much of the literature pertaining to supernatural topics is sensationalized and void of any scientific merit whatsoever. This book, I hope, is a rare exception. Although I am very much a skeptic in regard to supernatural phenomena of any kind, I attempt to remain open-minded. As the reader will note, I am completely baffled by some of the lights I have witnessed during eight years of North Carolina ghost light research. Though my intention was not to write a geography treatise, per se, clearly my disciplinary background is evident in the organization and presentation of information on the state's ghost lights and their legends. My primary objective in both research and presentation was to provide as much specific information as possible on the fifty-four lights that I identified within the state. The book can be thought of as a "how-to-do-it" manual to facilitate site visits and individual research by North Carolina residents and others who share an interest in this fascinating subject. Toward this end, each light—to the degree information is available—is presented with the following specific objectives in mind:

⚡ To *locate* the features as precisely as possible. Ideally, this will encourage readers to visits sites and encourage further observations and research;

- ✦ To *describe* the lights' appearance in as great detail as is possible based on my own observations and those gleaned from the literature;
- ✦ To *explain*, to the degree possible, the source/s of light;
- ✦ To *provide* as much detail as possible on the fascinating legend(s) associated with each light;
- ✦ To *identify* my own sources of information on each light, but also (when possible) to include additional sources for the interested reader to access. In the latter context a word of caution: many lights have a plethora of online descriptions, but much of the information appears to be spurious.

The book is divided into seven chapters, an introduction, five regional chapters, and a brief conclusion. Figure 1 is a map that shows the distribution, by county, of the state's fifty-four identified lights. Each of the regional chapters also includes a map that shows the locations in more specific detail. In this context, the reader must be cautioned that many accounts are extremely vague in terms of location. During the course of my research, I traveled an estimated twelve thousand miles within the state and visited most of the sites. Locations are given based on the best information available from the literature, online sources, and my own experience. I hope you find the lights and legends as fascinating as I have.

North Carolina
Ghost Lights and Legends

⚡ ⚡ ⚡

Chapter One

INTRODUCTION

⚡ ⚡ ⚡

"THERE IT IS!" The excited shout, uttered simultaneously by several college students and me upon sighting North Carolina's famous Maco Light, marked the beginning of my more than half-century fascination with and study of mysterious lights and their associated legends. There it was, a strange and rather spooky glowing orb floating above the railroad tracks near the old Maco Station on a cold, dark, slightly foggy night. What is it? What is the light's source? Why does it appear here and not elsewhere over the tracks? Our minds raced with these and many other questions as we searched in vain for answers to the seemingly inexplicable and rather spine-tingling phenomenon we were witnessing.

Few things are more apt to catch one's attention or prod a viewer's curiosity than the appearance of a strange light of unknown origin glowing in the distance. Mysterious lights appear throughout much of the world and have been reported for millennia. Millions of viewers have seen the peculiar specters and have been intrigued, bewildered, and occasionally terrified by them as they mysteriously appear, shine for a period of time, and then vanish into the inky darkness. Some float through nearby marshes or woodlands, whereas others reveal their eerie luminescence in distant vistas. They can flit like restless spirits through cemeteries, hover ominously above railroad tracks, or haunt isolated roadways where they often pursue and alarm unsuspecting travelers. These strange illuminations are known by many names, the most common being *ghost lights, spook lights, mystery lights*, and *Earth lights*. (Throughout the book, unless otherwise indicated, I refer to them using the generally accepted generic term *ghost lights*.)

All ghost lights share one thing in common: many, if not most, viewers are unable to identify their sources, and thereby assign them to the realm of supernatural or paranormal phenomena. To observers they appear as mysterious luminous entities that defy explanation on the basis of their knowledge. Because of their seemingly mystical nature, a fascinating and often hair-raising body of related folklore has evolved through time as viewers struggled to understand and explain ghost lights. In some instances, of course, lights and their related legends evolved as nothing more than imaginative spooky tales created to scare others with their eerie and possibly malevolent presence.

North Carolina's Ghost Light Tradition

With so many mystifying so-called paranormal features and conditions reported throughout the country, you might wonder why I selected ghost lights as the topic and North Carolina as the geographical setting for this book. The answer is simple. First, I have been fascinated by various arcane features and conditions for most of my life. But I must admit to never having seen, heard, or otherwise experienced a ghost, an extraterrestrial, a mythical creature, or a haunting voice speaking to me out of nowhere. I have, however, seen very strange lights in many locations throughout the country. Some strange lights, of course, readily yield to common-sense answers in regard to their nature and source. But many others—including a number of them in North Carolina—remain unexplained anomalies. In the pages of this book, I share with you my interest in and enthusiasm for the study of these intriguing features with case studies of the fifty-four ghost lights within the state for which I found one or more references.

In regard to the second part of the question, North Carolinians have a very long, rich, and diverse tradition of folk beliefs relating to mysterious places, enigmatic features, and strange events. Therefore, the state's dazzling array of ghost lights and associated legends is simply one of many categories of mystical phenomena and their associated folklore. In fact, it is probable that North Carolina leads the nation in its wealth of unusual, generally unexplained, and often rather frightening folk beliefs and tales. The suggestion is based on the large number of books, articles, and websites devoted to the state's various eerie features and their accompanying legends. In the introduction to his fascinating book *Weird Carolinas*, Roger Morley lent support to this belief in noting that North and South Carolina are "practically a world vortex for weirdness." There is scarcely a community in North Carolina that does not lay claim to some elusive ghost, strange sound, weird natural feature, creepy apparition, or gory legend.

Among the states, North Carolina also is home to the greatest number of ghost lights that either are today or once were visible, or at least said to have appeared at one time—about one-third of the nation's total. The state also can boast of having (or having had) several of the nation's most reliable, puzzling, and best-known ghost lights. The famous Brown Mountain Lights north of Morganton, for example, rank at or near the top of everyone's list of spectacular light displays. The same held true for the renowned Maco Light in Brunswick County west of Wilmington. Unfortunately, that mysterious glowing orb disappeared in 1977 when the railroad tracks over which it hovered for more than a century were removed. Several other sites within the state, although less well known, offer some of the nation's most spectacular and enigmatic ghost light displays.

One nagging problem I encountered in researching this book is the fact that some lights reported in the past are no longer visible, or at least have not appeared for a considerable period of time. This suggests the possibility that in some instances, at least, legends evolved independently in the absence of accompanying lights. As you will learn, a small number of lights (and associated legends) definitely are myths or hoaxes. However, I believe that in most instances if there is a legend, there was first a light—real or imagined—upon which it was based. Additionally, some legends far outlive the long-vanished lights with which they once were associated. This is not unusual; children today, for example, are familiar with nursery rhymes (inspired by folk tales) based on events that supposedly occurred centuries ago.

Several factors may help explain the state's many ghost lights and their related folklore. First, since the dawn of European settlement, North Carolina has had one of the nation's most densely populated rural environments. Nearly all ghost lights and their associated legends, as well as many other strange features and conditions, are found in remote rural areas where they are seen or otherwise experienced by the residents. And obviously, a strange light of unknown origin is much easier to spot in the relative darkness of a rural setting than in a densely settled and well-lighted urban area.

Second, in the distant past rural people were less apt to be well-educated than were their urban counterparts. In this context, it is significant to note that formal education did not become compulsory in North Carolina until 1907, long after most of the ghost lights were first reported. In the absence of science-based knowledge, people often turn to mythology for answers. As Carl Sagan noted in *The Demon-Haunted World*, "Pseudoscience is embraced . . . in exact proportion as real science is misunderstood." Lack of understanding, after all, provides a fertile seedbed of superstition in which myths and legends can germinate, take root, and grow. This hypothesis, in fact, may explain why a number of lights seem to have vanished, or at least lost their ghostly status. No doubt many of them still appear, but today's better-educated rural population is able to recognize their prosaic source such as vehicle lights in the distance. Additionally, as Sagan noted, a science-oriented society is much less apt to believe in supernatural or paranormal phenomena, or to accept accompanying bizarre legends, than is that which turns to mythology for answers.

Finally, cultural heritage certainly played a significant role. Most of the state's initial European settlers came from the British Isles. There, they possessed a rich and diverse tradition of mystical lore and storytelling forged in the fens, upland moors, woodlands, and waters of their homeland. Naturally, many of these traditions, including a belief in ghost lights, were part of the cultural luggage they brought with them to their new homes in North Carolina.[1]

Why Study Ghost Lights?

First and foremost, mysterious lights are intriguing; they kindle the imagination! Noted North Carolina author Nicholas Sparks capitalized upon this interest in his novel *True Believer.* The book's central theme revolved around a ghost light in a Pamlico County cemetery. (*Note:* To my knowledge, the county does not have any ghost lights.)

Upon learning that I planned to write a book on ghost lights, many friends and former academic colleagues thought I had lost my mind. Serious scholars, after all, do not believe in or pay serious attention to so-called paranormal or supernatural phenomena. As a result, they assiduously avoid that genre of perceived reality. In fact, as many scholars learned from personal experiences, studying "strange things" can be extremely hazardous to one's career. In fear of being labeled a "weirdo" (or worse), most academicians steer clear of any highly subjective topic that is even remotely judged to be mystical, ghostly, or in some other way bizarre. But who, after all, is to decide what is strange and should be off-limits, or, conversely, strange and fair game for scientific inquiry? To my critics, I simply ask, "What could possibly be worthier of serious scientific investigation than that mysterious realm of puzzling features and strange events that appear to lurk beyond the realm of existing knowledge?" After all, isn't shedding light on the unknown or unexplained the primary task of *all* scientific inquiry?

In this book I attempt to locate, provide a detailed description of, and—to the degree possible—offer a plausible explanation for North Carolina's mysterious lights. Although I am a geographer and scientist, the book is not intended to be a geographic or scientific treatise. Rather, it is the result of a long-standing personal fascination with enigmatic features, some of which lure me away from the secure tenets of science toward the shadowy realm of mystical phenomena. These investigations, I soon learned, would take me far beyond the familiar turf of my own academic discipline. Ghost light research spans a very broad range of subjects. Among the social sciences, research for this book drew extensively from anthropology, ethnology, folklore, history, and sociology; my investigation also involved extensive use of information from various physical sciences including physics, geology, hydrology, and meteorology. The spatial and temporal aspects of ghost light research fall squarely within the purview of geography and history. Ultimately, this study also drew me into the fascinating intersection of science, folk culture, and mythology.

An Organizational Framework

It is difficult to break six decades of academic tradition. With this in mind, I hope you will bear with me momentarily as I fall back upon my disciplinary heritage in order to better place this research in a meaningful framework. In simple terms, geography can be defined as the study of "What is where, why there, and why care?" in regard to the various features of Earth's surface. This definition lends itself well to the study of ghost lights and their legends. Let me explain.

In response to *What?*, I have identified and catalogued all of the state's ghost lights for which I could find information during more than six years of intensive research. As previously noted, some lights are or were actual luminous features that remain unexplained. Not all lights still appear, and in fact, some of them never did; rather, they were pranks, hoaxes, or other fabrications that through time evolved into local legends. Whereas I have identified fifty-four sites, the actual number could vary depending upon how one defines *ghost light*.

In regard to *Where?*, I have located the lights as precisely as possible based on available information, which, unfortunately, is often extremely vague, spurious ("fakelore"), or even lacking entirely. During the course of my research, I traveled an estimated thirteen thousand miles, visiting and conducting on-site studies of approximately three-quarters of the lights included in this book. Such visits are extremely important. They make it possible to place the features within a spatial and environmental context that, in turn, often sheds light (pun intended) on their source of illumination. The importance of location—the places, people, history, and natural environment—will become evident as you travel the state in the pages of this book and visit each of the various ghost light sites.

Of greatest importance in a scientific context is the question *Why there?* On a macro scale, I have already presented several hypotheses in an attempt to explain why so many ghost lights appear in North Carolina. Again, no other area of the country (or world) comes close to matching the state in its number and variety of mysterious lights and their related legends. At a more local level, the presence of a cluster of lights and similar legends often can be explained by the process of cultural diffusion. In this case diffusion refers to the spread of an idea—ghost lights—from place to place (much like the random spread of an illness) through time. Many legends, such as the Jack-o'-Lantern common to the northeast part of the state, for example, are mainly clustered within a relatively small area. Lights associated with railroad tracks and their most common associated legend are heavily concentrated in the southeastern area of the state. Both examples lend support to the importance of cultural diffusion as the primary agent in the spread and resulting distribution of an idea—in this context, ghost lights and their related legends. As would be expected, lights that mysteriously appear in a distant landscape are most common in the mountainous western part of the state, which offers broad panoramic vistas. On a micro scale, I attempt to explain the lights by searching for potential sources of illumination within their immediate environment. Additionally, location often relates directly to the substantial body of folklore that developed through time in reference to a light's nature and origin.

Finally, *Why care?* In answering this question, I am inclined to rely on the answer attributed to George Mallory when asked why he wanted to climb Mount Everest: "Because it's there." First and foremost, many of the lights, both past and present, remain unexplained; therefore, I believe they warrant serious attention by the scientific community. In this context, it is unfortunate that very little ghost light research is of a scholarly nature. Whereas I attempt to explain the source of some lights, an in-depth scientific analysis of each is beyond the purview of this book. Various researchers have conducted serious studies in an attempt to explain the nature and origin of many of the state's ghost lights. To my knowledge, however, most such efforts have failed to identify their sources. Further study certainly is warranted. It will, however, require a considerable amount of time, a team of serious science-oriented researchers, new approaches, and a variety of sophisticated equipment. This book locates and describes the state's ghost lights, which is an important first step toward a more comprehensive study.

At the local level, lights often play a significant role in promoting community and regional identity. Maco, for example, was never home to more than a small cluster of rural residents. Yet its name is recognized worldwide by people interested in ghost lights. Additionally, the magnetic attraction of such features often plays a significant social and recreational role. On a dark weekend night—particularly before the advent of TV and home computers—visiting a ghost light site was a popular and fashionable thing to do, particularly among teenagers. Even today it is not at all unusual to find a number of vehicles parked at the viewing site of a well-known light on a pleasant weekend evening. Finally, some of the better-known sites, such as Brown Mountain and its world-famous light display, have a significant financial impact on area communities. Visitors, after all, spend money for various activities and services.

On the negative side, those in search of lights are often guilty of trespassing (if planning to visit a light located on private property, always ask permission!), littering, and otherwise disturbing local residents. Ghost light seekers also place themselves in possible jeopardy when wandering about a remote location in the darkness of night. For example, there are numerous accounts of people shooting at strange lights, which could easily be the flashlight of some curious viewer rather than a "ghostly lantern" or "restless spirit" wandering about the countryside. And occasionally, as tragically occurred in 2010 at the Bostian's Bridge site near Statesville, someone hoping to see a ghostly event is killed. Each of the foregoing presents a potential challenge for law enforcement officers and certainly can try the patience of affected local residents.

Defining "Ghost Lights"

What is a "ghost light"? How are these enigmatic features defined? As you might expect, the task is somewhat more challenging than may appear at first glance. In fact, I am unaware of any widely accepted definition of mysterious luminous phenomena. A major problem, of course, is identification. Imagine two similar lights that appear in the distance. What makes one a "ghost light," whereas the other is just "a light"? It is possible that a viewer recognizes the source of one light but not the other. What about a second viewer who fails to recognize the source of either light, or still another observer who identifies the source of both? It is extremely important to remember that "ghost" is a perception of an individual viewer. Whereas lights are natural, ghosts, hence ghost lights, are products of the human imagination.

Are all unexplained luminous features ghost lights? Based on personal experience, I have seen supposed ghost lights at a number of the nation's best-known sites and immediately identified their source. There was absolutely nothing ghostly about them as far as I was concerned. On the other hand, judging from overheard conversations, I seemed to be alone among the many enthusiastic viewers at the various locations who believed they surely were witnessing something supernatural in nature. Generally speaking, I believe the following criteria adequately define the phenomenon:

1. The source of illumination remains a mystery, at least to some viewers.
2. Unlike randomly appearing lights, the light or lights appear repeatedly over a period of time, in the same approximate location, and with the same general appearance.
3. The light or lights are seen and reported by more than one individual and on more than one occasion.
4. Mystical explanations abound as the light (whether real or imagined) becomes entrenched in local folklore.

5. The lights, unlike UFOs, tend to be seen on or near the ground.

Actually, a number of the lights (or luminous legends) discussed in this book do not meet all five of my rather arbitrary criteria. I include them simply because at least one reference to each appears in the printed literature or on a website. Additionally, they are (or were) referred to as a ghost light (or a similar term) in local lore. And in most instances, a legend evolved to explain the luminous display. Hopefully, these guideposts satisfy the need to separate ghost lights from other perceived luminous (and also elusive) entities such as ghosts, UFOs, strange orbs appearing in photographs, or any other enigmatic luminous appearance.

Light Sources

As one would expect, a great many theories attempt to explain the sources of ghost lights. Some have scientific merit, whereas others are, well, unen*light*ening. The basic questions underlying all ghost light research relate to their nature and origin: What are they? What is their energy source? How and why do they differ in appearance? Why do they appear in a particular location and not others? Do they result from some unknown or unidentified natural energy source, or might they be caused by some mysterious paranormal agent? Skeptics, of course, maintain that all of them are of either human origin, such as lights of distant vehicles, or are caused by some natural agent such as swamp gas (also known as marsh gas), foxfire, or ball lightning. All hypotheses, regardless of how ludicrous they may seem to others, have their share of advocates.

In regard to the nature of the agent or agents responsible

for ghost lights, I am inclined to fall back upon the common-sense solution expressed in Occam's razor. This bit of folk wisdom basically states that when presented with several possible explanations, the simplest one is probably (although not always!) correct. In a not too hypothetical example, local folklore variously explains a mysterious light as being: the ghost of a soldier killed long ago in a bloody battle; the lantern of a railroad employee who was decapitated in a tragic accident and is destined to spend eternity searching for his severed and lost head; the ghost of a person searching for a mysteriously vanished lover; or (rarely) lights of vehicles traveling on a distant highway. Faced with these options, it seems most plausible to accept the hypothesis of vehicle lights. It is important to remember, however, that anything that occurs begs an explanation. The answer may be simple, fully conforming to existing knowledge or common sense. On the other hand, a light can defy explanation, at least based on its appearance and the viewer's knowledge—including, in some instances, teams of scientists.

For readers interested in a very detailed description and analysis of natural lights, a topic that is beyond the purview of this book, I recommend William R. Corliss's splendid volumes, *Remarkable Luminous Phenomena in Nature*, and Chapter 1, "Luminous Phenomena," in *Handbook of Unusual Natural Phenomena*. Corliss documents more than 120 natural light sources, not all of which, of course, relate to ghost lights. Dozens of theories attempt to explain strange luminous phenomena. Some of the more common (and plausible) include the following: atmospheric conditions resulting in ball lightning; optical illusions created by temperature inversions that reflect and distort distant lights; flammable swamp and marsh gasses, phosphine (PH_3) and methane

(CH_4), bursting into flame when released into the atmosphere (commonly referred to as "Will-o'-the-Wisp," *ignis fatuus*, or "Jack-o'-Lantern"[2]); foxfire, a bioluminescence resulting from certain types of glowing fungi; piezoelectric charges caused by light-creating seismic activity affecting quartz or other crystalline rocks; and light displays that result from activity within Earth's electromagnetic field.

Finally, in keeping with the insight offered by Occam's razor, some ghost lights clearly are nothing more than lights from distant settlements, cars or trucks, trains, planes, or some other familiar source. Rarely, however, do True Believers accept, or for that matter even consider, these matter-of-fact and most obvious agents as a light's possible cause. In this context, we are reminded that the enigmatic is far more fascinating and exciting than is the mundane.

Everyone, it seems, loves a mystery. As a scientist, however, I must admit to being a hardened skeptic in regard to the possibility of lights emanating from any supernatural agent. Nonetheless, as previously mentioned and as you will soon learn, a number of North Carolina's lights do remain a baffling mystery to me and to numerous others in terms of their nature and possible source of illumination. And certainly it is this aura of mystery that makes ghost light research both challenging and exciting. In regard to the lights discussed in this book, I explain what can be explained and readily acknowledge the failure of my research when in doubt. In other words, I accept as fact only that which I have personally experienced or for which reliable information exists from trusted sources.

In all instances, my data and hypotheses can and should be tested by further investigation. So when I suggest a probable light source—such as parking lot security lights in a distant community—readers are encouraged to visit the site and draw their own conclusions regarding its nature and cause. After all, I might be wrong! Additionally, many sites have multiple light displays. What I saw might be only a small portion of a much greater and more varied light spectacle. This, no doubt, is particularly true of railroad-associated lights, several of which—based on descriptions and what I have personally witnessed—offer a mystifying variety of luminous features. As is true of all research, it is essential that those involved in ghost light research keep an open mind, although as Art Bell, long-time host of the radio program Coast-to-Coast AM, once quipped, "not so open that your brain falls out."[3]

Ghost Light Research

In some ways studying ghost lights is like panning for gold. The vast majority of material through which one must sift in search of a precious nugget is extraneous. And as often as not, the glistening piece of metal that finally appears in the pan turns out to be nothing more than iron pyrite—fool's gold. True nuggets are scarce, widely scattered, and rarely found. So it is with much of the information pertaining to ghost lights. Hopefully, this book is an exception; think of it as a "how-to" manual for visiting ghost light sites where you are encouraged to do your own exploring and to draw your own conclusions. In a sense, it represents a pioneering effort, inasmuch as it is the first work that attempts to present a comprehensive and detailed listing, description of, and—to the degree possible—explanation for, all known ghost lights within a single state.

Gold, of course, is not found by sitting in the comfort of one's home and reading a book about panning for the precious metal, and so it is with experiencing ghost lights. The best way to study them is to do as I did during the research for this book—visit sites. First, however, one must learn something about ghost lights and their most important characteristics. Important things to look for include the following:

⚡ **Location.** Where, specifically, is the illumination seen? In what direction(s) does one look from the viewing site? Is the phenomenon visible from more than one location or direction? Does it always appear in the same place? If lights appear in multiple locations, are they fixed in place, or do they appear in various random positions? Where is the light located in relation to possible sources of illumination? Location is the single most important factor in studying ghost lights, because it can offer clues that help explain their sources.

⚡ **Movement.** If a light moves, how far, how fast, and in what direction(s) does it travel? Is the movement repetitive, always following the same path, or is it random? Many lights, particularly those resulting from distant vehicles, are revealed by their location relative to a roadway, their appearance (generally white or red), and the direction and duration of their movement.

⚡ **Appearance.** How often are the lights seen? Do they appear only at a certain time or under particular environmental situations (e.g., season of the year, atmospheric conditions, phase of the moon, or time of night)? Do all lights look the same, or do they vary in size, shape, color, and duration of appearance (as well as location and movement)?

↯ **History.** When did the light first appear, under what conditions was it first seen, and who (if known) first reported a sighting? Of all information pertaining to lights, that pertaining to earliest sightings is most apt to be spurious. For example, if a prosaic source such as automobile headlights is suggested for a particular light, almost always the date of "first sighting" is pushed back in time in order to exclude the commonsense explanation and retain the mysterious aura of the phenomenon.

The significance of each of the foregoing factors will become more evident as they are considered in the context of individual lights discussed in the book.

In ghost light research, absolutely nothing can substitute for onsite visits to assess a light's environmental setting and perhaps witness the light display itself. If you do not believe it is feasible to visit a particular location at night, I urge you to go during daylight. As often as not, once you see the site, you will be able to at least place the light in its environmental context. This, in turn, can help you identify a possible source. In discussing the lights, I provide as specific information as possible about their locations and appearances. Many lights are in remote locations; again, you can decide yourself whether a nighttime visit is advisable. Fortunately, the state's major light displays are visible from public and seemingly safe vantage points.

Another advantage of site visits is seeking out people from the area who are familiar with a light and its accompanying legend. I have found that most local residents are intrigued by my ghost light research. Some, of course, think I am loco; they never heard of a strange light in their area and wonder where I came up with such a nonsensical idea. Others seem reluctant to discuss a ghost light in their neighborhood, believing, no doubt, that such a belief is passé in the modern era. And, of course, there are those who do not want their neighborhood—or in the case of police, their area of jurisdiction—overrun by curious ghost light seekers. Many folks, however, are delighted to discuss lights and their ghostly legends. During the course of this research, I met or otherwise communicated with hundreds of wonderful people who were fascinated by the research and were more than willing to share their thoughts and experiences on the subject.

Ghost lights appear in a variety of geographical settings. One commonality shared by nearly all of them, however, is a remote and therefore "scary" location. Who, after all, is going to be scared out of their wits over the sighting of a strange light seen in the distance from the intersection of Second and Main? If the primary purpose of an outing is to freak someone out, or to frighten one's self, the more isolated and spooky the location the better. Only a small number of lights occur near a community or in a densely settled rural area.

About half of the state's ghost lights are associated with roadways or railroad tracks. The latter settings, in particular, are intriguing. Twenty-two railroad-associated sites either have a light display now or did at one time according to the information available. Amazingly, these lights appear in a dazzling array of colors, sizes, shapes, motions, and locations relative to the rails. In fact, of those I have seen in North Carolina (and elsewhere), no two are alike. The underlying reasons for this incredible diversity remain an intriguing and as yet unsolved mystery. Lights generally appear at a considerable distance down the tracks, although according to some accounts they can get close enough to actually touch or pass the viewer. Some railroad-associated lights are stationary, and others are as spectacular and varied as a Fourth of July fireworks display. A small number of lights are or were associated with water bodies, swamps, or marshlands in which they create an eerie, glowing presence. And a few, such as the Brown Mountain Lights and those seen from Thomas Divide Overlook on the Blue Ridge Parkway, are seen moving about within sweeping vistas that cover a vast area of rugged terrain.

When conducting ghost light research, one quickly learns that significant differences often exist among various eyewitness descriptions and the actual appearance of a particular light. A discrepancy also exists in many instances between what I have seen and what others claim to have witnessed. You should think of ghost lights as you would a Rorschach inkblot test—even though the same object is seen by many observers, how it is interpreted and described can and generally does vary considerably. Many factors influence what one "sees." They include past experience, culture and ethnicity, formal and informal education, religious beliefs, and a host of other views that one holds.

It is often said that "seeing is believing." The statement, attributed to St. Thomas in the mid-1690s, suggests that only tangible evidence—something physical, or concrete—can be convincing. This philosophy, however, begs the question: What is "tangible"? Do we believe what we see, or do we see what we believe? In other words, do they (in this case, ghost lights) appear as *they* are, or do they appear as *we* interpret them to be in terms of our individual belief systems? As applied to ghost lights (and perhaps all other purported supernatural or paranormal phenomena as well), I believe that the latter condition almost always holds true: we see what we believe, want, or expect to see. Unfortunately, ghost light researchers tend to be divided between the starry-eyed believers in some paranormal agent and closed-minded debunkers. As is true of all research, it is best to approach the question with an open mind while searching for hard evidence upon which to base one's hypotheses.

Not surprisingly, supernatural theories abound and are discussed in the context of those lights to which a mystical source is attributed. Viewed in this context, if one sees something that he or she *believes* to be supernatural, almost certainly that is how it will be interpreted. To those so predisposed, a light emanating from a most ordinary source suddenly becomes a spooky, mystery-shrouded, paranormal phenomenon. For example (and I have witnessed this on many occasions), when people of differing mindsets see lights at a distance down a lonely stretch of railroad track, some viewers immediately recognize the lights as those of vehicles crossing the tracks on a distant road. As seen by the True Believers, however, the light is perceptually transformed into the lantern of a revenant—the common legend of a railroad employee who searches in vain for his head, which was severed in a tragic (and rarely documented) accident and never found. It seems that many people *want* to believe in paranormal phenomena simply because doing so adds an air of mystery and excitement to their otherwise rather humdrum existence.

Luminous Legends

I am absolutely amazed, as I'm sure you will be, at the number of truly imaginative legends developed through time in association with the various lights. Frankly, I find these often bizarre folktales much more fascinating than I do the more matter-of-fact explanations. Legends are examples of folk-lore that may be widely believed and supposedly are based on historical events that remain unconfirmed by evidence. Most of them exist in that twilight zone between events that possibly could have occurred and those that never happened outside the realm of imagination. A classic North Carolina example is the tragic railroad accident described in the above paragraph. Such an event certainly could have happened. But to attribute a ghost light to the ghost of a decapitated revenant is a bit far-fetched. The key to a good legend is its plausibility, to which considerable "spin" is almost always added.

Legends are spawned in response to several catalysts. Some owe their origin to tales that evolved in support of various political, social, or religious beliefs. These legends developed with an ulterior motive. With but few exceptions, I find little if any evidence of such influences in the case of ghost lights. Rather, luminous legends appear to have evolved through time in response to three primary agents: fears, fascinations, and functions.

Several of the state's ghost light legends clearly relate to peoples' fears, particularly during the early years of settlement. In the northeast region of the state, for example, a fear of densely wooded pocosins (swamps; various spellings) and the heinous things—both real and imagined—that lurked within them, gave rise to several eerie legends. The woodland-lurking Jack-o'-Lantern (ignited swamp gas), for example, was widely believed to lure viewers to their deaths. In those locations where strange, unexplained lights actually appeared, people were naturally fascinated with them. Often, they also were genuinely terrified by the strange luminous phenomena, the source of which they did not understand.

The great majority of legends seem to have evolved in response to peoples' fascination with something they observed but were unable to explain. As is true of the famous Brown Mountain Lights, for example. They have been seen for perhaps centuries, yet I find no reference to anyone ever having feared that light display; rather, viewers are fascinated by them. Most of the numerous accompanying legends, regardless of how far-fetched they may seem, were attempts through time to explain the strange array of lights that generally appear above and beyond the low mountain.

Finally, some ghost light legends evolved to serve a function. Many, for example, obviously were designed to scare viewers. In this context, it is important to realize that during the mid- to late-20th century, the vast majority of viewers seem to have been teenagers out for a thrill. Even the headless revenant wandering about with his lantern is involved in the function of searching for his head.

Surprisingly, despite the state's incredibly rich and varied tradition of ghost light legends, folklorists have paid very little attention to this genre of folklore. The only detailed study I found during years of research on the subject is a 1973 article by Gary Hall that appeared in *Indiana Folklore*. It is generally regarded to be the landmark work on the subject. In his study of "The Big Tunnel," a railroad tunnel located between Fort Ritner and Tunnelton, Indiana, Hall identifies a number of ghost light legend motifs and variants, not all of which apply to North Carolina's lights.

North Carolina Ghost Lights

A comprehensive list of North Carolina's identified ghost lights appears in Table 1. The listing is in alphabetical order by community and includes location by region, community, county, name of light, and the type of environment in which the light appears (or appeared). In the body of the text, rather than following the alphabetical list in presenting the state's lights, I have used a regional organizational format. This will make it easier for you to visit sites when traveling through a particular area of the state. Arbitrarily, and in order to have a relative balance in the number of lights in each of the areas, I divided the state into five regions (Map 1): the **Northeast** (north of US Highway 70 and east of I-95); **East Central** (east of I-95 and between US 64 and I-40); **Southeast** (south of US Highway 70 and east of I-95); **Central** (west of I-95 and east of I-77); and **Western** (remainder of the state west of I-77). The following five chapters locate, describe, and assess the lights and accompanying legends found within each of these areas.

North Carolinians can take justifiable pride in the state's magnificent array of natural splendors, its complex and fascinating history, the wonderful hospitality of its people, and its delightful variety of places and regions. This book spotlights yet another facet of North Carolina's many superlatives—its rich and intriguing tradition of ghost lights and their related folklore. The following pages take you on a journey through the state in search of its mysterious lights and luminous legends. Additionally, during your travels you will be introduced to many of the state's communities and rural settlements that gave birth to the mysterious orbs and their fascinating associated tales. Of greatest importance, I hope that you are able to see many of the lights yourself and thereby gain a greater appreciation for how and why they have lured, fascinated, and mystified viewers for generations. Enjoy your journey!

TABLE 1. North Carolina Ghost Lights

Region	Community	County	Name of Light	Environment
NE	Ahoskie/Aulander	Hertford	Early Station	Railroad
NE	Ahoskie/Cofield	Hertford	Brantley's Grove	Cemetery
C	Badin	Stanley	Old Whitney Train Track	Railroad
EC	Bear Grass	Martin	Swinson's	Swamp
W	Big Laurel	Unknown	Unidentified	Unknown
W	Blowing Rock	Watauga	Unidentified/Historical	Terrain
SE	Bolivia	Brunswick	Half Hell	Roadway
W	Cedar Mountain	Transylvania	Green River Preserve	Terrain
NE	Chapanoke	Perquimans	Chapanoke/Four Mile Desert	Swamp
W	Cherokee	Swain	Thomas Divide Overlook	Terrain
W	Chimney Rock Pass	Rutherford	Historical Sighting	Terrain
SE	Clarkton	Bladen	Buie	Railroad
NE	Cofield/Winton	Hertford	Buffaloe's	Spring
NE	Columbia	Tyrrell	Death/Doom	Cemetery
C	Concord	Cabarrus	Campbell's Ghost	Railroad
EC	Conetoe	Edgecombe	Unnamed	Railroad
NE	Conway	Northampton	Devil's Poquosin	Swamp
EC	Cove City	Craven	Cove City	Swamp
C	Craven	Rowan	File's Store	Cemetery
W	Cullowhee	Jackson	Wahehutta (1)	Terrain
W	Cullowhee	Jackson	Wahehutta (2)	Terrain

TABLE 1. (*continued*)

Region	Community	County	Name of Light	Environment
C	Durham	Durham	Catsburg Ghost Train	Railroad
C	Eden/ Wentworth	Rockingham	Berry Hill	Railroad
SE	Evergreen	Columbus	Evergreen	Railroad
SE	Fair Bluff	Columbus	Causey's Road	Railroad
EC	Fremont	Wayne	Fremont Railroad	Railroad
W	Hewitt	Swain	Mud Cut	Railroad
EC	Hookerton	Greene	Hookerton Railroad	Railroad
W	Hot Springs	Madison	Shut-In-Creek	Terrain
EC	Jamesville/ Dymond City	Martin	Dymond City	Railroad
EC	La Grange	Lenoir	Bear Creek	Swamp
SE	Maco	Brunswick	Maco	
SE	Mintz	Sampson	Mintz	
NE	Momeyer	Nash	Momeyer	Railroad
W	Morganton	Burke	Brown Mountain	Terrain
EC	Ocracoke	Hyde	Teach's	Water
EC	Pactolus	Pitt	Pactolus	Railroad
W	Plumtree	Avery	Slippery Hill	Cemetery
W	Rutherfordton	Rutherford	Gilboa Church	Cemetery
NE	Seaboard	Northampton	Devil's Racetrack	Roadway
NE	Seaboard	Northampton	Ephraim's	Swamp
EC	Smithfield	Johnston	Mill Creek Bridge	Roadway bridge
W	Statesville	Iredell	Bostian's Bridge	Railroad bridge

TABLE 1. (*continued*)

Region	Community	County	Name of Light	Environment
W	Statesville	Iredell	Unnamed	Railroad bridge
SE	Stedman	Cumberland	Stedman	Railroad
NE	Tarboro	Edgecombe	Tarboro	Railroad
C	Union Grove	Yadkin	Forbush Road	Terrain
SE	Vander	Cumberland	Vander	Railroad
C	Wendell	Wake	Morphus Bridge	Roadway bridge
SE	Whiteville	Columbus	Old Tram Road	Roadway
NE	Williamston	Martin	Hanging Tree	Swamp
EC	Williamston	Martin	Screaming Bridge	Roadway bridge
SE	Wilmington/ Fayetteville	Various	Mt. Misery Road	Roadway
C	Yadkinville	Yadkin	Phantom Headlights	Roadway

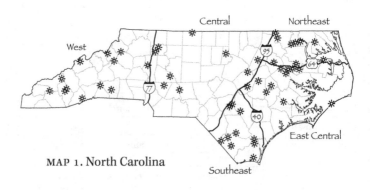

MAP 1. North Carolina

Chapter Two

NORTHEAST

↯ ↯ ↯

T HE NORTHEAST IS one of the oldest European-settled areas of the state, with permanent settlement dating back to the late 1650s. Therefore, it is not surprising that many of the oldest reported ghost lights and their accompanying legends illuminate the region's folklore. The relatively low-lying area offers a landscape mosaic featuring slow-flowing, cola-colored streams, brackish estuaries, scattered woodlands, and cleared farmland. Much of the agricultural land owes its origin to the region's extensive drainage reclamation projects. When Europeans first occupied the area, they were overwhelmed by nature. Settlers were surrounded by dense woodlands and foreboding pocosins, the regional term for swamps (var.: poquoson; poquosin). In their European homeland, such environments were widely feared judging from the many legends that depicted them as the habitat of dangerous creatures, both mythical and real, and malevolent spirits. Immediately, they set to work clearing land for settlements, fields and pastures, and trails. But as these human-created landscapes expanded, beyond their immediate periphery always lurked the dark and sinister unknown. It was an environment extremely conducive to imaginations—and fears—running rampant. Here, more than any other region within the state, the natural environment played a significant role in ghost light lore.

Northeastern North Carolina is home to eleven ghost lights and their accompanying legends, including at least several that are visible today. The amazing display of lights seen from Early Station Road between Ahoskie and Aulander certainly ranks among the nation's least known yet most dazzling and unexplained ghost light spectacles. Several of the state's most gripping ghost light legends also evolved here as local residents attempted to explain the area's strange luminous sightings and unnerving events. In some respects, the region's lights and related legends are unique. For example, unlike elsewhere in the eastern part of the state, only three of the eleven lights are associated with railroads. As might be expected, based on the area's often turbulent history, a number of the lights and legends date back to the harsh era of slavery, or to the time of the Civil War. And here, in an area first settled by British colonists more than three centuries ago, we also find several legends with almost certain direct links to Old World origins. We begin our exploration of the state's ghost light sites with a visit to Early Station Road, which, if putting on its usual show, does a spectacular job of introducing you to the fascinating subject of ghost lights and their associated legends.

TABLE 2. Northeast NC Ghost Lights

Community	County	Light	Environment
Ahoskie/Aulander	Hertford	Early Station	Railroad
Ahoskie/Cofield	Hertford	Brantley's Grove	Cemetery
Chapanoke	Perquimans	Four Mile Desert	Swamp
Cofield/Winton	Hertford	Buffaloe's	Spring
Columbia	Tyrrell	Death/Doom	Cemetery
Conway	Northampton	Devil's Poquosin	Swamp
Momeyer	Nash	Momeyer	Railroad
Seaboard	Northampton	Devil's Racetrack	Roadway
Seaboard	Northampton	Ephraim's	Terrain
Tarboro	Edgecombe	Tarboro	Railroad
Williamston	Martin	Hanging Tree	Swamp

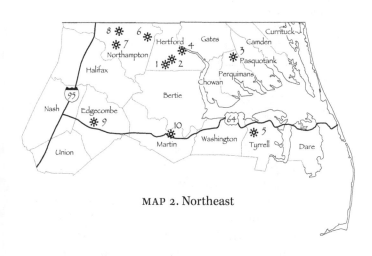

MAP 2. Northeast

Ahoskie/Aulander (Hertford County):
Early [Earley/Early's] Station Light (railroad)

This often spectacular display of lights is best seen from where Early Station Road crosses the tracks of the old Seaboard Coast Line (now NC-VA) Railroad. The road branches off NC 42 in a southerly direction at Poor Town, about 1.5 miles west of Ahoskie, and crosses the tracks in another 1.5 miles. At the crossing, look westward down the tracks toward Brick Mill Road (approximately 2 miles) and Aulander (about 5 miles). The lights seem to appear on the viewer's side of the distant road.

During the past half century, I have seen many of the country's better-known ghost lights. But absolutely nothing could have prepared me for the remarkable display of lights seen during my two visits to Early Station Road. Most ghost light sites have their own characteristic display; that is, what is seen is always somewhat similar. But here lights present a stunning, kaleidoscopic array of varied colors, motions, sizes, shapes, and positions relative to the tracks. They are also quite reliable. The lights have put on a dazzling show, with as many as a dozen strikingly different appearances, during each of my visits. Reportedly, lights dance above the tracks throughout the night and appear year-round, although some reports suggest that they are most active in the early evening during summer months.

The Early Station Lights may, in fact, be the nation's best-kept ghost light secret. Surprisingly, no mention of them appears in any of the comprehensive national lists.[1] Furthermore, very little information pertaining to the lights exists in the literature or online, and amazingly, I spoke with a number of local residents who were unaware of their existence.

Brick Mill Road looking toward Aulander. Lights as seen
from Early Station Road appear in this area

Before describing any ghost lights, it is important to understand the environment in which they appear. Lights, of
course, must have some cause, of which many possibilities
exist. Yet the immediate area offers none of the usual possible sources of illumination such as swampy conditions,
buildings, power lines, or other structures. There is, however, a light source that may confuse many viewers. Looking westward, at a distance of about two miles, Brick Mill
Road crosses the railroad at a northwest/southeast angle. It
is probable that some viewers are confused by the lights of
vehicles that appear briefly as they cross the tracks. Headlights of southbound vehicles and taillights of those north-
bound are clearly visible. These lights, however, are easily
recognized as they differ greatly from the "real" lights. They

are roughly identical in their appearance, direction of movement, and duration of appearance. In fact, both the lights and the vehicles are clearly visible when seen at dusk.

Descriptions of the lights vary greatly. Based on their descriptions, no two of several dozen viewers who shared their experiences online seem to have seen the same thing. This confirms the display's amazing diversity. According to a local resident, when one looks west down the track, a bright light may appear. Other viewers, many of whom are anonymous, described the phenomenon as a single white light that appears to maintain the same intensity, size, and distance; a light resembling that of an oncoming train, or what looks like a flashlight in the distance, but about eight feet in diameter when it reaches the viewer. A trusted informant, James Allen, saw the light and described it as "A bright flashlight, [which] moved across the tracks, from side to side. It then disappeared, only to appear again a moment later as a light facing us, before disappearing again." What is most interesting about these descriptions is that the viewers all saw bright *white* lights, and in each instance the lights behaved in a somewhat similar manner.

In his book *Ghosts of the North Carolina Shores*, Michael Rivers describes the light as follows: "Since the 1920s, a single light has been seen along the edge of the tracks, rising and stopping in the center of them. The light then begins to move. It neither floats nor bounces as it makes its way down the tracks, seemingly toward you." Rivers describes the light as being yellow/orange in color and about the size of a basketball. Some other witnesses also describe lights appearing in various colors.

During my visits to the site I have never been disappointed.

During my first viewing in 2012, a number of lights appeared. Several were bright white flashes seen for a second or two just above and near the tracks and much closer to Brick Mill Road than to my vantage point. About the time I was convinced that all lights had the same appearance, a pink glow appeared high in the trees to the right (north) of the tracks. It remained visible in the same spot for perhaps twenty seconds before it slowly began to fade away. No sooner had it vanished than an orange ball of light about the size of a basketball suddenly appeared. It hovered over the tracks for perhaps five seconds before it slowly dimmed and vanished. Surprisingly, none of the lights that I saw appeared to move up or down the tracks. But one bright white light did move in a spectacular way—like a Roman candle, it shot straight up, well above the tree tops, and out of sight.

During my second visit, a variety of lights once again presented an absolutely amazing display. A yellow light that looked much like the beam of a flashlight appeared on the left side of the tracks, zigzagged its way down the rails for a short distance, and disappeared. Several minutes later, a bright white light appeared to the right and slightly above the tracks. It blinked off and on numerous times over a period of several minutes. During much of the time this light was visible, a small yellow light appeared to shine right on the tracks at a short distance in front of it (toward the viewer). Finally, a faint red light—that looked as though it was shining through a fog—appeared above and to the left of the rails. It fluttered from left to right through the trees before slowly fading out of sight. The variety of colors, shapes, and sizes, locations relative to the rails, and movements make it extremely difficult to identify a possible energy source for the Early Station

Lights. Based on my experience, however, this is one of the country's most extraordinary and as yet unexplained ghost light displays.

As is true of so many of North Carolina's railroad-related lights, legend holds that a railroad worker was decapitated in a terrible train wreck (which remains undocumented, as are nearly all such tales) and his severed head was never found. He is now engaged in an eternal search for his lost head, and the lights, of course, are said to be from his swaying lantern. One might question how a headless revenant is able to see—that is, be able to benefit from the lantern's light in his search—but I will leave this strange paradox to the reader's imagination.

A second legend, which as far as I know is the only one of its kind in the United States, appears on the "North Carolina Ghost Guide" website. It tells of two trains traveling in opposite directions on the track between Ahoskie and Aulander. Conductor James Pearce set the brake of his train and awaited what was certain to be a thunderous and deadly impact. Suddenly, to his amazement, the onrushing engine and cars veered away. As it passed by, Pearce was shocked to realize that it was a phantom image of his own train. Railroad policy required that he file a report at the next stop, which happened to be Early Station. Evidently, and for reasons unexplained, the report was not finished. As you might imagine, while at the station Pearce took a lot of good-natured ribbing over his sighting of a "ghost train." After saying goodbye to his friends at the station, he and his train vanished into the night. Little did his friends realize that tragically his goodbye would be final. According to the legend, Pearce's train jumped the tracks, and he was killed. The light, seen swinging back and forth and getting brighter as it approaches

Early Station only to vanish as it reaches the road crossing, is conductor Pearce's lantern as he returns to the depot to complete his unfinished report. Inasmuch as there never was a depot at Early Station, this account seems most unlikely. The nearest station was three miles down the tracks in Ahoskie.

According to Rivers, the Army Corps of Engineers spent several weeks investigating the lights sometime during the 1960s. They were unable to determine a source and concluded that their findings were inconclusive because "none of the properties or values [are] consistent with a natural phenomenon." Variously, the literature suggests (and dismisses) swamp gas, ball lightning, and lights emanating from some human source (other than the lights of vehicles crossing the tracks on Brick Mill Road, of course).

Based on my own experience with dozens of ghost light sites across the country, the Early Station display is, indeed, both spectacular and extremely mystifying. What I have seen truly does defy explanation. There may, however, be some clues. For example, according to most accounts they are seen only when looking toward Aulander, whether from the Early Station Road crossing, or when walking down the tracks toward Brick Mill Road. And according to most accounts, they seem to appear only at a distance, perhaps within a half mile of the distant road. I have not seen any lights close-up (other than dozens of bright fireflies on a muggy summer evening). The relationship between the lights and the rails remains a mystery. But several US lights, including the famous Maco Light (chapter 4), vanished when the tracks were removed. This suggests a possible relationship between the metal rails and the mysterious illuminations. Perhaps some as yet unexplained electromagnetic force is responsible. One thing is certain: where there is light, there must be an energy source.

Here, however, the source of energy and its relationship to the strange light display remains unknown.

The viewing site is located in a populated rural area and is on a well-traveled road. The lights are fascinating, and despite some assertions to the contrary, I found them in no way threatening. Ahoskie is located just a few miles away and offers all basic visitor services. If you visit the site, almost certainly you will be treated to what I believe to be one of America's most spectacular and mysterious, yet surprisingly little known, ghost light displays.

Ahoskie/Brantley's Grove (Hertford County): Ball of Fire (cemetery)

Brantley's Grove is a small rural settlement located about three miles northeast of Ahoskie, near the intersection of Ahoskie/Cofield, Willoughby, and Vann Roads. Jenkins Cemetery is on Wood Lane about five hundred feet east of its intersection with Ahoskie/Cofield Road.

In *Ghosts of the North Carolina Shores*, Michael Rivers relates a fascinating story about a light reportedly seen on occasion during the first half of the twentieth century. As is true of several lights in North Carolina, this one is associated with a cemetery, which adds a spine-tingling element of spookiness to its appearance. Unfortunately, Rivers's account is the only reference I have found that describes the strange ball of fire that supposedly haunted the area of Brantley's Grove for decades. And local memories of the light are dim, no doubt because its last reported appearance was more than six decades ago.

As Brode Denning told the story (presumably during the 1960s), many years ago a ball of fire rose as a ghostly apparition from the ground of Jenkins Cemetery. Then, moving at a height of about ten feet above the ground, it floated through a wooded area, across a field and dirt road, and struck the side of a house. As though it had fulfilled its mysterious fiery objective, the light then returned to the cemetery and vanished. Brode claimed to have seen the ball of flame "off and on all my life."

In another sighting several months later (year unknown), he reported that the flame moved in a similar manner, following a path nearly identical to that previously reported. It rose like a restless spirit from the cemetery, but this time appeared much brighter than before. The light then passed through the wooded area, again crossed the field and dirt road, and hit the porch of Percy Jenkins's house. As happened previously, the light then returned to the cemetery and disappeared. Soon thereafter, the resident of the apparently targeted house, Percy Jenkins, died. Whether his death was related to the light, as some local residents believed, no one will ever know. Mysteriously, after Jenkins died the light was never seen again. In some respects, the account of this light coincides with the British folklore described in some detail in the context of Columbia's Light of Death (or Doom), discussed later in this chapter, and several other ghost lights within the state.

Over the years, a number of people have attempted to explain the strange flame. Among the theories are foxfire (a bioluminescence caused by several species of fungi), a Jack-o'-Lantern (swamp gas), and ball lightning. Foxfire can be ruled out, simply because it is stationary: moss doesn't move! Both the swamp gas and ball lightning theories are extremely doubtful inasmuch as the light supposedly appeared on numerous occasions and followed the same path. Decades have passed since its last reported appearance, which makes it difficult to know the specific nature or possible cause of the strange illumination. Since he was the only reported observer, could the light possibly have been nothing more than a restless ghost given birth in Brode Denning's fertile imagination? Unfortunately, we will never know.

Chapanoke (Perquimans):
Four Mile Desert Light (swamp)

Four Mile Desert Road is northeast of Winfall, located on NC 37, just north of US 17, and southwest of Parkville. Take Two Mile Desert Road Northeast out of Winfall to Swamp Road, a distance of about two miles. There, after a slight jog to the right (east), it continues as Six Mile Desert Road. The road crosses what once was the southern edge of the Great Dismal Swamp.

As its name suggests, Dismal Swamp is a dismal and foreboding place that inspired many ghostly legends. Among them are eerie lights that seem to haunt various parts of the enormous wooded wetland. The best-known lights were those that appeared along Four Mile Desert Road where the narrow, sandy (hence "desert") trail passed through the dark and menacing swamp. Many nighttime travelers on the lonely stretch of road were startled to see lights described as white or bluish in color and up to several feet in diameter. They rose ghostlike from the murky swamp waters and hovered just above the surface as they moved slowly through the trees. Occasionally, the light hovered over the roadway, where it appeared to chase startled—and often panicked—travelers for some distance. Having completed its ghostly mission, like a vampire seeking protective darkness, the mysterious light returned to the swamp and vanished.

As you would expect, the lights spawned many gory legends, most of which date back a century or more. One early and rather horrific story involved a female bear that snatched a child from a buggy as it crossed the swamp on Four Mile Desert Road. A posse was formed to search for the child, who was never found, and to find and kill the bear. Deep in the swamp, they found a dead bear cub that had been shot. The mother bear, locals believed, simply took a human life in revenge for the loss of her cub. After others gave up the search, the child's father pressed on, going ever deeper and deeper into the swamp from which he never returned. The light is said by some to be from the lantern carried by the grief-stricken father who still wanders through the dark and threatening swamp in search of his lost child.

Another more recent tale is a fairly common urban legend. It tells of a husband and wife who were crossing the swamp on Four Mile Desert Road when a tire went flat. After replacing the tire, the husband got back into the car only to find that his wife was gone. As the story goes, he turned white with terror when he saw his wife's limp body hanging from a nearby tree. According to local legends, the light is either the ghost of the woman, or the ghost of the man now searching for his dead wife's killer.

In a swampy environment the most logical source of strange lights is marsh gas. In support of this theory, during the mid-1980s this portion of the Dismal Swamp was drained, and the woodland was cleared for farmland. Sandy Four Mile Desert Road still crosses the area, but apparently no unexplained lights have appeared since 1986. Today the area produces crops rather than ghost lights and their accompanying legends.

Cofield/Winton (Hertford County):
Buffaloe's Light (spring)

A light is said to have appeared at a spring located on River Road one mile north of the Wiccacon River. The actual location of the spring is unknown.

In his book, *Illuminating the Darkness*, Dale Kaczmarek includes Buffaloe's Light as one of fifty-five ghost lights within the entire United States. One would think that this inclusion suggests a rather significant phenomenon. Unfortunately (and inexplicably), all of the information presented by Kaczmarek was taken verbatim from F. Roy Johnson's 1966 book, *Legends and Myths of North Carolina's Roanoke-Chowan Area*. Johnson neglected to cite his source of information.

"Buffaloe" was the name given to deserters during the Civil War. According to legend, Confederate soldiers captured a Buffaloe, whom they shot. The deserter, however, did not die from the wound. Not wanting to waste another musket ball and more powder, the struggling soldier was taken to a nearby spring and drowned. According to Johnson, "Occasionally since that time people have reported seeing a bright light floating in the vicinity of the old spring."

No one in the vicinity with whom I spoke could, well, shed any light on this legend. The area is swampy, and it is possible that a light, if indeed one ever existed, was swamp gas (*ignis fatuus*).

Columbia (Tyrrell County):
Death Light/Doom Light (cemetery)

An unknown location, near an unnamed cemetery, at an unspecified place in Tyrrell County.

I have found only two sources that describe an eerie ghost

light event that reportedly occurred somewhere near the community of Columbia during a brief period in 1904. Mysteriously, after its deadly appearances over a span of several nights, the light or lights never appeared again. No one living in the area today seems to be aware of the events described in the two accounts. Under these circumstances, you might logically wonder why I include Tyrrell County's "Light of Death" (or "Doom"). After all, it is more than a century old and remains unverified. Reference to the events appears here for three reasons: first, the tale does a splendid job of spotlighting a number of problems that confront anyone who attempts to study ghost lights and legends; second, although I am unaware of any other light in the country that closely corresponds to this particular tale, the motif of a ghost light foretelling death is fairly common; and third, the theme of the associated legend can be traced directly to British folklore.

The earliest known reference to Tyrrell County's death-foretelling light appeared in the *Raleigh News & Observer* in April of 1965, fully sixty-one years after the events supposedly occurred. The article was written by Mrs. W. H. Booker, at the time a resident of Columbia. Booker indicated that the story came to her from a relative of the family involved, with names withheld by request (as so often is the case and, of course, rendering any follow-up impossible).

In Booker's version of the tale, a family consisting of father, mother, and son was stricken with typhoid fever. As they were unable to function on their own, neighbors took turns caring for them. One evening while sitting on the home's front porch, the assisting neighbors witnessed a strange light that appeared to move about over a nearby cemetery. The light flickered and grew brighter but vanished when the observers entered the cemetery to investigate its source. The next morning, they were shocked to find the father dead. The following evening, the same scenario played out, although now the light was much brighter, so bright in fact that the inscriptions on headstones were legible. Once again the observers entered the cemetery in search of the light's source, but, as happened the previous night, it simply vanished as they approached. The next morning, they found the mother dead. As the legend goes—well, do you want to guess the events of the following night and early morning? If you guessed a replay of the two previous nights, with the son found dead in the morning, you are beginning to understand how a legend such as this evolves! The group gathered the fourth night to watch for the light, but it never appeared again (perhaps because the family ran out of members?). Booker ended the story by noting that "No one has ever explained the phenomenon."

A second and somewhat similar account appeared twenty-seven years later in Catherine T. Carter's 1992 book, *Ghost Tales of the Maratoc.* By now, you are familiar with the story, although Carter's version is different than Booker's in some respects. In this rendition the light did not appear on consecutive nights, and it was members of three *different* families who died. Inexplicably, this account—although given eighty-eight years after the reported event and with not a single source of information cited—relates very specific details. For example, Carter describes an evening during which "[A] slight breeze was stirring from the direction of a nearby creek, and that was the only thing that made the torrid summer night bearable. There wasn't much conversation, just the buzzing of the ever-present mosquitoes and the squeak of the rusty porch swing." It seems a bit strange that Carter could provide such an incredibly detailed description of conditions, yet failed to mention names, locations (other than

Tyrrell County), dates, or other useful information pertaining to the alleged events.

One aspect of the "Light of Death" (or "Doom") legend is unique. Most tales are spawned and grow as attempts to *explain* lights. In this case, however, the legend is built around the light's effect—foretelling death. According to Janet and Colin Bord, a somewhat similar folktale was commonplace in Britain. There, legend held that a "corpse light" would visit a home to presage an impending death and then follow the same path that the corpse would later take on the way to the burial ground. In the Tyrrell County version, no mention is made of the light visiting the home, but it did move about within the cemetery and foretold the death of area residents.

So, what does this legend illustrate? To begin, there are (to my knowledge) only two accounts of the described events. Although both occurred in the same general location and time frame, there are significant differences in regard to what supposedly happened. Neither account gives a location other than "near a family graveyard" and "a nearby creek." As many readers know, family cemetery plots are very common throughout rural North Carolina. It is therefore difficult, if not impossible, to identify a specific site and check headstones for names and dates of death. North Carolina did not keep death records until 1913, so it is impossible to verify either story with official data. Reference to a nearby creek in soggy Tyrrell County offers no clue to location. As a detailed map clearly shows, the area has many swamps and winding streams. Neither account mentions names of any individuals involved. Specific dates, other than 1904, are not indicated. In other words, neither story gives any information that might provide a lead to further investigation of the alleged deaths or their associated legends. As is true of many ghost light tales, there is ample reason to believe that the lack of particulars is deliberate. Who, after all, wants boring details to interfere with the telling of a good story?

Conway (Northampton County):
Devil's Poquosin (swamp)

The Devil's Poquosin (now largely drained) was located east of present-day NC 35 between Conway and Milwaukee. It extended for a distance of about two miles, including present-day Panther Swamp.

Pocosin is a regional term for swamp, a low-lying, thickly wooded area with occasional standing water. During the early period of settlement, as the name implies, Devil's Poquosin was a place to be avoided by area residents. It was a haven for panthers, wildcats, bears, and potentially deadly water moccasins. There were even reports of weird creatures believed by some to be witches, or possibly even the devil himself in disguise. With each telling, the stories became wilder and the legends of the Devil's Poquosin grew more sinister. There are far too many ominous (and imaginative) tales to relate here. Every teller, it seems, spun his or her own yarn.

In colonial days the British settlers in northeastern North Carolina believed in "Jack-o'-Lanterns." Unlike the Halloween pumpkins, these were mysterious lights that usually appeared deep within a wooded area. The idea of a Jack-o'-Lantern as a ghost light appears to have originated in Ireland. It spread to England, from where it was introduced into North Carolina, probably during the first half of the 1700s. As you can imagine, if people avoided the swamp, the devil, witches, and other demons lurking within needed to devise a way to lure them into their clutches. As a result, according to legend, the lights appeared along the edge of the pocosin on a fairly regular basis. Occasionally, someone was drawn into the swamp out of curiosity and became lost. Fortunately, at least as it pertained to local residents of the time, I found no reference suggesting that anyone ever died from such a misadventure.

Much of the land once within the pocosin was drained long ago, and many decades have passed since the light last appeared. There may, however, be a logical explanation for the lights as described. Jack-o'-Lanterns go by several other names, including Will-o'-the-Wisp and swamp gas. Some scientists believe that the flickering lights, which appear as a flame in swamps and marshes, are caused by marsh gas or swamp gas (*ignus fatuus*). Rotting vegetation releases methane and phosphine which, when united, can ignite and flame briefly. That said, the thought of witches, demons, and the devil himself trying to lure unsuspecting passers-by into their ghoulish clutches makes a much more fascinating and scarier story than does a theory of burning swamp gas!

Momeyer (Nash County):
Momeyer (railroad)

Momeyer is approximately five miles west of Nashville on 64A. Tressell Loop Road branches off 64A in an easterly direction between Annie Leigh way and Jackson Road just east of town. In about one mile, the road turns abruptly to the right and in a very short distance crosses the tracks. Lights reportedly appear when one looks eastward down the tracks.

At one time, a strange light that appeared over the railroad tracks looking east from Tressell Loop Road drew many curious viewers to the site. People came from miles away for a chance to see an eerie illumination described as being whitish in color and floating above the tracks. In *Best Ghost Tales of North Carolina*, which is the primary source of information for this particular story, Terrance Zepke quotes Rocky Mount resident William McIlwean who was a frequent visitor to the site. He claimed to have seen the light twenty-seven times in fifty visits over a span of years. Although I find no recent reports of sightings, it is difficult to know whether it is because the light has vanished or, as Zepke suggested, people simply are no longer interested. It is possible, of course, that the lack of interest may be attributed to the fact that the light's source is now recognized.

There are several possible explanations for the light. First, some as yet unidentified source of illumination is associated with many tracks, including more than twenty in North Carolina alone. Whereas there are a number of theories that attempt to explain the relationship, none of them is entirely satisfactory. Second, Little Sapony Creek flows beneath the rails a short distance down the tracks. It is possible that the light is from ignited marsh gas (Will-o'-the-Wisp). This, however, seems unlikely inasmuch as McIlwean saw the light on more than half his visits to the site. A third explanation seems to be favored by local residents. Just west of Nashville is an infrequently traveled road that is in direct line with the tracks. At a distance of several miles, the headlights of vehicles traveling westward would appear as a single white light.

Oh, yes, and there is a fourth hypothesis: the ghost of a railroad worker who was decapitated—his head was never found, and he is in an eternal search for the lost skull. The light is from his swaying lantern. As mentioned previously, this is a very common tale with which you will become quite familiar as you travel the state via the pages of this book in search of ghost lights and associated legends. If, however, the light no longer appears, could it be that the revenant simply gave up his futile search?

Seaboard (Northampton County):
Devil's Race Track (roadway)

Devil's Race Track Road extends from NC 305 at the south edge of Seaboard (Elm Street) eastward to Mount Carmel Road, a distance of approximately four miles.

The Devil's Race Track legend appears to date from the Revolutionary War era, but beyond this period, information becomes a bit hazy. Several centuries ago, the area through which today's Devil's Race Track Road passes must have been a densely wooded, dark, and foreboding place, an ideal environment to stimulate imaginations. Today, and quite probably for many decades, the only tangible link to early events is the (now) paved roadway. Otherwise, the happenings that contributed to its name have long vanished from collective memory. There has been no report of a strange, unexplained light appearing along the road since the mid-twentieth century.

Again, F. Roy Johnson's 1966 book, *Legends and Myths of North Carolina's Roanoke-Chowan Area*, appears to be the sole reliable source of information for this light. And much of his narrative is based on tales told by a single informant, J. G. Bottoms of Margarettsville, who was born in 1875 (there is no mention of when or how the information was obtained). Bottoms claimed that the heavily traveled road was in very poor condition, resulting in accidents, many of which were fatal. Because of its sordid reputation, the road earned the name Devil's Race Track. According to Johnson, Bottoms also suggested that the road was difficult for horse and buggy travel but was "easy for the Devil in whatever form he chose, to flash along the way at breakneck speed." Evidently, many travelers claimed to see the devil racing along and "[t]he strange phenomenon included the appearance of lights." This is the only reference I have found to ghost lights in association with the Devil's Race Track.

Dale Kaczmarek, citing only Johnson, succinctly summarized the numerous name-origin legends: "Ghost lights have been reported in the narrow part of the roadway where so many people allegedly lost their lives while engaged in racing and drinking—a dangerous mixture." Seaboard, located at the west end of Devil's Race Track Road, reportedly had the only bar in a rather large area. Many of the tales involve drinking in excess and the resulting drunken behavior, particularly racing along the treacherous stretch of road after having "one [or more] for the road." Perhaps the lights were more a product of excessive indulgence in spirits, rather than ghostly spirits appearing as luminous orbs?

Seaboard (Northampton County): Ephraim's [Ephriam's] Light (uncertain)

Other than near Seaboard, the location of Ephraim's Light remains unknown. Despite a lengthy search, I have not found any information that confirms the location of a Woodruff Plantation in Northampton County.

Ephraim's Light is extremely interesting for a reason typical of so many such features: *What story, if any, should one believe?* The legend has some strange—and certainly gruesome—twists. Local tradition holds that Ephraim, a slave on the Woodruff Plantation, killed his master, Martin Woodruff. Other than hearsay and one state government report, no record of the murder seems to exist. Here, however, the story diverges into several variants of the legend's motif.

According to one source, knowing that his days were numbered as a result of his heinous deed, Ephraim hanged himself. Another tale indicates that he was captured and hanged by a lynch mob. Still another source states that he was captured by a posse, tarred and feathered, and burned at the stake. And yet another intriguing report, which appeared in *Historical Documents of Genealogical Interest to Researchers of NC's Free People of Color* (January 30, 1861), indicated that the North Carolina legislature approved a bill to "pay Evans Ferguson and Ben Smith, free persons of color, of Northampton County, $400, the reward by the Governor for the apprehension of Ephraim, a slave, for the murder of his master, Mr. Woodruff." This report, however, makes no mention of what ultimately happened to Ephraim. Considering the conditions and passions of the time, any of the foregoing seems plausible. Based on the government report, however, it does appear that sometime prior to 1861, probably in or about 1860, a man named Woodruff was murdered by a slave, Ephraim.

Soon after Ephraim's death, various people began to report the appearance of a strange light. Some described it as flickering, whereas others referred to it as a fire or flame that appeared on occasion near the (never identified) spot where Ephraim was burned at the stake. Those who believe this version of the story suggest that the light is either the flame of his pyre, or "his flame," suggesting that Ephraim's restless and vengeful spirit lives on. In an interesting and relatively recent twist, J. M. Pressley gives a much different version of the light's location and appearance. He refers to an "eerie yellowish light that occasionally appears in the downstairs windows [of the supposed, but unidentified, Woodruff Plantation home], seeming to flutter and dart from room to room before vanishing."

Details of Ephraim's Light and its associated legends appear to have vanished from the memory of area residents. Extensive research failed to identify a location or, for that matter, the former existence of a Woodruff Plantation in Northampton County. It is highly possible, of course, that the light never existed at all, other than as local lore. However, because of the record of government payment for Ephraim's capture, we know that a slave named Ephraim and a Mr. Woodruff did exist. We probably will never know whether the gruesome tale grew from a Will-o'-the-Wisp, some other illumination of unknown origin in or near an old plantation house, or simply as a baseless legend from the collective imagination of the time. Nonetheless, the event as described does serve as a grisly reminder of a very troubled and turbulent bygone era of American history.

Tarboro (Edgecombe County):
Tarboro Spook Light (railroad/urban)

Raccoon Branch Road and McNair Road (off Howard Avenue) cross the CSX railroad tracks about three and two miles, respectively, west of Tarboro. From either crossing, look eastward down the tracks toward town.

Although a number of references exist to a spook light seen near Tarboro, all of them appear to be based on a single account. The only detailed description I have found to the Tarboro Light is a sighting described by an individual identified only as "James" that supposedly occurred in 1980. When looking eastward down the tracks from a vantage point west of Tarboro, he and some friends claimed to have seen an eerie orange-colored, globe-shaped light they estimated to be three feet in diameter. It appeared not to "shine" or cast a shadow. The light seemed to hover at a constant height of two to three feet above the railroad tracks at a distance of several hundred yards. But here the description abruptly ends. As James told the story in his brief account, the light began to move menacingly toward him and his companions. Unnerved by the rapidly approaching, ghostly glowing orb, they jumped in their vehicle to flee the scene. But you can imagine their horror when the car lights dimmed and the engine died. Eventually, the car started, and they wasted no time in leaving the area. Rattled by the experience, James claims never again to have returned to the site at night.

It is most unfortunate that no other information exists on this light. James's description is almost identical to the Maco Light that I witnessed in the early 1960s: both similar in color, neither shining nor casting a shadow, both round in shape and several feet in diameter. The glowing orb remained at a constant height above the tracks. When approached by a viewer, it backed away; if the viewer backed away, the light menacingly followed. This suggests that what James and his friends claim to have seen was a light created by some as yet unidentified relationship between metal rails and the occasional appearance of an eerie illumination.

I visited the Tarboro site on three occasions and, unfortunately, did not see anything that remotely resembled the light that James described. However, a number of moving lights are visible as vehicles turn off Anaconda Road and cross the railroad tracks that run parallel to and just north of the street. Lights also are visible from vehicles crossing the railroad on the US Highway 64A bridge at the western edge of Tarboro. Additionally, there is an intriguing stationary yellow light that hovers above the tracks at a distance, which somewhat resembles the glowing orb that James described. I went in search of this light's source and found that it is two very bright security lights (that appear as one from a distance) in a parking lot near the in-town intersection of North Main and Howard Avenue.

Perhaps we will never know what James and his friends witnessed that night in 1980. But at least a visitor to the site will see lights shining from various sources. And who knows, it is entirely possible that one of them—as described by James—may be an eerily glowing ghostly orb of unknown origin that mysteriously floats above the railroad tracks.

Chapter Three

EAST CENTRAL

⚡ ⚡ ⚡

T
HE NATURAL LANDSCAPE of East Central North Carolina is dominated by low-lying coastal plain, Pamlico Sound and its associated rivers and estuaries, scattered woodlands, and numerous pocosins. As is true of much of the Middle Atlantic Seaboard region, it is also pocked with Carolina bays, mysterious elliptical lakes and earthen scars of ancient, but unknown, origin. It is easy to imagine that much of the area was quite threatening to the early European settlers. Bath, a small community founded in 1705 on the north shore of Pamlico Bay, is the state's oldest permanent European settlement. Most of the region was settled by the end of the eighteenth century and thereby shares with the Northeast the distinction of being the state's oldest area of European habitation.

Early settlers immediately set about the task of clearing the land, converting its native forest cover and soggy wetlands into productive farmland. For decades, the East Central region has been the state's leading producer of tobacco, a crop of which North Carolina has long led the nation in production. Although tobacco acreage has declined somewhat during recent years, agriculture continues to be extremely important to the region's economy. In addition to a growing diversity of crops, the area also boasts a number of huge hog and poultry operations.

Eleven ghost lights dot the East Central region's luminous landscape and folklore, several of which date from the early period of European settlement. A direct link exists, for example, between tales nurtured in the British homeland and the region's five ghost lights that reportedly haunted the area's swamps. Another five lights appear, or once appeared, in association with railroads, which initially penetrated the area during the last half of the nineteenth century. One, Teach's Light, is said to appear in the murky water of Pamlico Sound. Today, most of the lights seem to have vanished, or appear only rarely. But their often gruesome legends live on and thereby provide a fascinating link to past perceptions, fears, and imaginations.

TABLE 3. East Central NC Ghost Lights

Community	County	Light	Environment
Bear Grass	Martin	Swinson's	Swamp
Conetoe	Edgecombe	Unnamed	Railroad
Cove City	Craven	Cove City	Swamp
Fremont	Wayne	Fremont RR	Railroad
Hookerton	Greene	Hookerton RR	Railroad
Jamesville	Martin	Dymond City	Railroad
La Grange	Lenoir	Bear Creek	Swamp
Ocracoke	Hyde	Teach's	Water
Pactolus	Pitt	Pactolus	Railroad (tracks removed)
Smithfield	Johnston	Mill Creek Bridge	Swamp/bridge
Williamston	Martin	Screaming Bridge	Swamp

MAP 3. East Central

Bear Grass (Martin County):
Swinson's Light (swamp)

Bear Grass is located on Bear Grass Road about eight miles south-southwest of Williamston. Bear Grass Swamp borders Travis Creek just south of the small community.

The legend of Swinson's Light is of unknown origin. As the tale is told, it pre-dates the American Revolution. It is a legend some elderly residents of Bear Grass claim to recall, but the only details I have found appear in a single written account. In 1980, the "Skew Arkians," students in the Junior Historical Club of Bear Grass School, published a book, *Weird Tales of Martin County,* in which one entry was the "Legend of Swinson's Light." That source, which the students themselves claimed to be mere speculation, provided all of the following information.

As they told the story, in 1761 the Earl of Granville gave nine hundred acres of land bordering Bear Grass Swamp to a local resident, John Swinson. Evidently, Swinson was a man of means who supposedly buried his wealth at some unknown location on the property. After he died, some residents claimed to see a strange light in the swamp. The light was described as a large ball of fire that only appeared at certain unspecified times of the year. It was very bright and moved about at treetop level. Reference to a large ball of fire suggests burning swamp gas as the possible source of flame, although this hypothesis cannot explain a very bright light among the treetops (if, indeed, this description is correct).

According to the accompanying legend, the light is Swinson's ghost "guarding his buried treasure." The students indicated that in the 1970s a few elderly residents of Bear Grass still claimed to have seen the mysterious light as youngsters. During recent decades, however, both memories of the phantom light and the light itself seem to have faded away. But who knows, perhaps gold and precious jewels still await discovery by some fortune seeker who is lured into the shadowy swampland bordering Travis Creek by the ghostly flickering of Swinson's Light.

Conetoe (Edgecombe County):
No known name (railroad)

Conetoe is located at the intersection of US Highway 64A and NC 42. The light, when visible, is viewed by looking southward down the tracks from the rail crossing on Highway 42.

The Conetoe Light is interesting for several reasons. First, it is the only light that appears fairly regularly in the East

Track at Conetoe

Central region. Despite the reliability of its appearance, however, I found only two extremely brief, anonymous, and relatively uninformative references that relate directly to the phenomenon and, unfortunately, both of them are worded identically. They state: "Reports of a strange light on the tracks, believed to be the spirit of a girl who died there 100 years ago." Just beyond the point the tracks turn eastward and in line with them, is a house with windows facing the viewer. Unfortunately, there is no way of knowing if the light that is visible today was the source of the initial sighting.

With so few leads to follow, I was sure that research on this light would lead to a dead end. The accounts failed to indicate a location or direction in which to look other than "on the tracks." One additional source, seemingly as an afterthought, totally dismissed the Conetoe Light, suggesting that quite likely it is confused with the light reportedly seen along the tracks near Tarboro (chapter 2). In 2012, I passed through Conetoe one afternoon, talked with several lifetime residents, and found no one who was aware of a "ghost light" in or near the community. Discouraged, I moved on believing that there was nothing more to see or to learn.

More than a year passed before, out of curiosity, I decided to follow-up on the Conetoe Light using one of the most important ghost light research tools, Google Earth's satellite imagery. I found that about two miles south of town the CSX tracks turn sharply to the left (east). Much to my surprise, a house is located several hundred feet beyond the curve and directly in line with the tracks as viewed from in-town crossings. During my next research trip, I returned to Conetoe and found that the house has two windows that are in line with and slightly above the tracks. With lights on in either room, their glow appears to the distant viewer to be strangely hovering just above the rails. I can only guess that this is the source of light that some believe to be the spirit of a young girl who reportedly died more than a century ago, long before the light first appeared.

Cove City (Craven County):
Cove City Ghost Light (swamp)

Cove City is a small town at the intersection of NC Route 41 and old US 70. Great Dover Swamp is located between the community and Trenton. Reportedly, the best viewing spot was from the third bridge on NC 41 south of Cove City. The light is said to have appeared just across the border in Jones County.

For more than a century, many travelers passing through the Great Dover Swamp between Cove City and Trenton experienced an odd and bewildering sight that often terrified the startled viewers. They saw a strange light most often described as an orange, basketball-sized ball of fire. As you would expect, descriptions of the eerie glow vary greatly. Some observers reported seeing a thirty-foot-diameter orange ball of flame that resembled a full moon. Other reports describe a light that appeared at a distance and simply wandered aimlessly about the swamp. Several travelers claimed that it appeared to chase their car, or even race past it, and in some instances it is said to have actually passed through their vehicle, or so close that it shook.

Many theories were advanced to explain the nature and source of the Cove City phenomenon. According to author Daniel Barefoot, whose work on the light is the most detailed, nearly a dozen so-called "scientific" explanations exist. They range from alien spacecrafts to hoaxes, and secret government weapons to fireworks and fireflies. There is, however, one rather significant clue: evidently, the lights vanished in the late 1970s when the swamp was drained and the area was converted to farmland. This suggests ignited swamp gas as the most probable source, and one that fits most (but not all) descriptions. When the swamp was drained, the flammable methane and phosphine gasses were no longer released.

The Cove City Light is extremely interesting for another reason—the motif of the legend that evolved to explain the phenomenon. It closely parallels the Chapanoke/Four Mile Desert Light legend (chapter 2), making it one of only two examples of this theme of which I am aware in the entire United States. This legend begins with hunters killing a bear cub, which leads the mother bear to snatch an infant traveling by buggy through the swamp. In the Four Mile Desert Light legend, it is the missing infant's heartbroken father who endlessly searches the swamp for his child with a lantern (the source of the light). The Cove City Light legend only differs in that it is the brokenhearted mother who still wanders the swamp in search of her lost infant.

Fremont (Wayne County):
Fremont Railroad Light (railroad)

The easiest access to the viewing site is to take Highway 117 north from Fremont for 2.5 miles to Aycock Acres Road. Follow this road eastward about 1 mile to where it crosses the CSX railroad tracks. Look southward toward Fremont. (*Note*: Local residents reportedly do not take kindly to trespassers, and there are "No Parking" signs near the frequently patrolled viewing area.)

As is true of so many such features, the Fremont Railroad Light remains an elusive mystery. Descriptions of the light vary considerably with numerous contradictions (examples of which appear in parentheses). Supposedly, on dark summer (or cold, foggy, winter) nights, a red light appears as one looks southward down the tracks toward Fremont. Some describe it as a swaying (wobbling or bobbing) light above the tracks that may (or may not) move closer to (or farther from) the viewer. According to one anonymous source, however, a number of local residents claim the light chases them and that "if [it] catches you, you could die!"

Strangely, there are more legends that explain the light than descriptions of the light itself. Most tales follow the theme of a person killed by a train. In one version, a local drunk was killed and decapitated by a train, and his head was never found. The light, as is so common to this genre of explanation, is the lantern (or cigarette, or cigarette lighter) of the victim who still searches for his lost head. In a different version, one night a man was pushing his bicycle along the tracks and was struck by a train. The light, some say, is from his bike as he attempts to finish his now eternal journey.

A recurring theme in ghost light lore is that of vehicles being unable to start when a light appears. In the *Ghosts of America* website, a person identified only as "Heather" tells of such an experience: "[P]ark your car at the railroad tracks . . . when you try to crank your car it won't start. But go back in the morning and it starts right up!" (I hope she did not suggest parking on the tracks and leaving your car there for the rest of the night. The CSX tracks are still used.)

While conducting research on the Fremont Light, I communicated with a number of local residents. To briefly summarize their input, there are many rumors about lights and sightings, but very few facts or actual sightings. Strangely, no one with whom I communicated had ever gone—or, for that matter, seemed willing to go—to the road crossing a short distance north of town to see if a light actually appears. In a somewhat similar vein, Aaron Moore, a newspaper reporter who grew up in the area, indicated that he heard stories about the light for years but never saw it himself. He considered doing a story on the light but found little local interest in the subject when talking with Fremont residents. His experience coincided with my own: he was unable to find anyone who had actually seen the light.

I visited the site in 2012 but was advised by a law enforcement officer not to go there alone after sundown. Additionally, parking is prohibited where Aycock Acres Road crosses the tracks. The officer also indicated that he had not seen anyone parked near the tracks in years. As described, it seems likely that the red light is (or was) either a railroad signal light, a stationary red light in town, or, as one resident suggested, the tail lights of vehicles traveling southward on a Fremont street that parallels the tracks. It is interesting that there is no mention of a light appearing when someone within the community looks northward along the railroad right-of-way. This suggests that the source of light (if it exists) is either in or very near town and/or faces only northward. Inasmuch as the light evidently is no longer seen, perhaps it was never anything more than a glowing red spark of imagination, or, more likely, an illumination that local residents were able to easily identify. Of course, it is possible that the reluctance of local residents to check out and report on the light rests in the belief that if it catches you, you could die!

Hookerton (Greene County):
No known name (railroad)

Hookerton is located on NC 123, about five miles south of Maury. The light's location is unknown.

The Hookerton railroad light, as reported, is a classic example of the incredibly vague information that so frequently confronts the ghost light researcher. Although mention of the light appears in numerous sources, I found but a single description of it, which is widely copied by others. Unfortunately, the information provided fails to indicate the original source, makes no reference to dates, and contains no helpful information in regard to the light's location. Yet, surprisingly, the legend has morphed into a rather widely reported ghost light occurrence.

All accounts that I have found read as follows: "It is said that if you go to that old train railroad in [*sic*] you will see some woods and if you go in very deep and flick your car lights three times a young man will come out *with a lantern* [emphasis mine] and paralyze you." The tale continues to note that "for this to happen you have to turn of[f] [*sic*] your car and get out. The story is that a man was waiting for his wife and a train came and ran over him."

No one in Hookerton seems to be aware of the legend or its origin. What I find most interesting in regard to the tale is that the Hookerton lantern is one of only a dozen railroad-related lights listed within the entire United States by the comprehensive website, "Haunt Jaunts." Yet of the twenty-one railroad lights I have identified in North Carolina alone, there is less information for this light than any other.

The accompanying legend is also interesting in that a man waiting for his wife was killed by the train. This is a recurrent theme. In this instance, however, there is no mention of what the lantern-carrying man is searching for or doing, let alone why or how he supposedly paralyzes anyone who enters his ghostly realm.

Jamesville/Dymond City (Martin County): Dymond City Light (terrain)

Dymond City is a ghost town site. Easiest access is to take NC 171 south from Jamesville approximately 3.5 miles. About

0.75 miles past Farmlife, turn left (east) on Dymond City Road and follow it for about 3.5 miles. The settlement was located at the point where Dymond City and J & W (Jamesville-Washington) Tram Roads intersect.

Detailed information on the Dymond City ghost town site appears in Catherine Carter's book, *Ghost Tales of the Moratoc*, and several websites. The community grew and gradually withered away during the latter decades of the nineteenth century. It was a railroad town located on the old J & W Railroad. The train, locally known as "Jolt and Wiggle," made one round trip each day. When the railroad shut down operations in 1894, the community withered away rapidly, and in 1927 a fire destroyed everything that remained of Dymond City other than distant memories.

Writing in 1992, Carter indicated that "Older residents who live nearby tell stories about the lights that can be seen in Dymond City on dark and moonless nights." But the settlement was long gone by that time, so her reference to "in Dymond City" is unclear. She later notes that after the town site returned to wilderness, "People began to talk of seeing a light that bobbed along where the old tracks once ran. It was most often described as a lantern held in someone's hand—an unseen hand that guided the light as it bounced along." Other anonymous sources, writing online in recent years, describe "a little orb that danced from one side of the street to the other. [I]t went from looking like a gold orb . . . into looking like a red burning fire." Another anonymous writer described what appeared to be a bright light that flashed. Still others described what appeared to be a ball of fire moving about just above the treetops. Judging from the diverse descriptions, it is possible that the same energy source and light phenomena seen from Early Station Road between Ahoskie and Aulander (chapter 2) occurred here while the tracks were still in place.

Local lore suggests that the lights may be the ghosts of various railroad personnel, or even the ghost of a surveyor who, according to legend, did his work at night with a torch (which seems most unlikely). It does seem that some strange luminous phenomenon did—and perhaps still does—appear along the old J & W Railroad right-of-way. In this context, it is important to note that the rails were removed long ago. As is true of several other ghost light sites in the state, it is entirely possible that at one time a relationship did exist between the rails and their associated lights. Further, this is a swampy environment, and the several references to flame-like lights also suggest the possibility of ignited swamp gas as the source. Finally, a number of back roads crisscross the area, and it could very well be that at least some of the lights reported are those of distant moving vehicles.

LaGrange (Lenoir County):
Bear Creek Jack-o'-Lantern (swamp)

LaGrange is a small crossroads community located at the intersection of US 70 and NC 903, midway between Kinston and Goldsboro. Bear Creek crosses US 70 about a mile west of the town, flows southward roughly paralleling Bulltown Road, and flows into the Neuse River about 5.5 miles south of LaGrange.

David Barefoot, in *North Carolina's Haunted Hundred,* Vol. 1, *Seaside Spectres,* relates a fascinating tale told by a witness who claimed to have seen a light at some undisclosed time during the first half of the twentieth century. While fishing alone along Bear Creek, James Creech saw a distant light. As described, it was "two feet wide and one foot deep." It rose to a height of about fifty feet, floated for some distance, paused for a moment, and finally faded away into the woods.

Evidently, Creech was but one of many area residents to witness a Jack-o'-Lantern in the swamp bordering Bear Creek. During the second half of the twentieth century, much of the land bordering the creek was reclaimed for agriculture, resulting in very few, if any, recent sightings. This factor alone suggests that the light probably was swamp gas.

Ocracoke (Hyde County): Teach's Light (water)

Teach's Hole is in Pamlico Sound, a short distance southwest of the Ocracoke community. Sightings also have been reported in various areas of Pamlico Sound and in the open Atlantic off Ocracoke Island.

The infamous pirate Edward Teach (aka Blackbeard) terrorized Atlantic and Caribbean shipping during the second decade of the 1700s. He made many raids from his favorite hideaway—Teach's Hole. As one might expect, Blackbeard and his exploits provided the colorful and often horrific background material for countless tales, including numerous grisly legends that became staples of North Carolina's rich body of folklore. One such folktale—and perhaps one with a thread of truth as a luminous phenomenon—is Teach's Light.

According to well-documented historical accounts, Blackbeard was killed in a fierce battle with British forces in November of 1718. He was decapitated, and his head was hung from the bowsprit of the victorious Royal Navy vessel. The rest of his body was unceremoniously dumped into the dark waters of Teach's Hole. Since that time, there have been numerous reports of strange lights observed both above and within Pamlico Sound and adjacent waters. It is said that they are the ghost of Blackbeard searching for his severed head.

It is entirely possible, if not probable, that strange lights do appear occasionally in Pamlico Sound and the adjacent Atlantic. In his book, *Remarkable Luminous Phenomena in Nature,* William Corliss documents more than a dozen sources for phosphorescent marine displays. And above-water lights also have numerous possible sources (including, according to locals, Blackbeard searching for his head).

Since the mid-twentieth century, as is true of so many ghost lights, reports of sightings have become increasingly infrequent. Perhaps the spirit of Blackbeard simply became tired of the futile search and finally gave up. Or, more likely, today people are less inclined to believe in paranormal explanations of strange luminous phenomena. According to Charles Whedbee and several other writers, however, there may be still another reason. According to Whedbee, "When Teach's lights are seen, either above or below the surface of the water, it always portends a disaster of some sort [including the death of friends, relatives, or even the viewer] for the ones who see them." This could be reason enough to turn a blind eye to any strange nocturnal lights appearing in the murky water of Pamlico Sound.

Pactolus (Pitt County):
Pactolus Light (railroad—tracks removed)

Pactolus is located 9 miles east of Greenville at the intersection of highways US 264 and NC 30. From town, take NC 30 north for 4.5 miles to Carl Morris Road. Turn left (west) on Carl Morris Road and go 0.5 mile to the former railroad right-of-way (located just before a power line crosses the road). A

Pactolus with old RR tracks removed

light reportedly was seen when one looked northward along the (now removed) railroad tracks. The land is now private property, and the trail is blocked by a gate and pile of dirt.

A wealth of information exists on the Pactolus Light. Unfortunately, as is true of so much ghost light literature, most of it is incredibly vague, extremely confusing, and often highly contradictory. It is almost certain that at one time *something* luminescent appeared when one looked northward along the tracks at the point Carl Morris Road crosses the former railroad. And it is possible that sightings continued for at least a short period of time after the rails were removed in the early 1980s. Most reports posted during the past several decades, however, suggest that either the light has vanished, or that it appears very infrequently. The former railroad right-of-way is now overgrown with vegetation, which severely restricts visibility. I believe this factor alone explains the absence of recent sightings.

Descriptions of the light vary considerably. Stewart Edwards described it as "a fast white streak of light . . . head high . . . about the size of a golf ball which shoots across the path like a shooting star and then other times it lingers in the path for almost minutes, hovering and changing colors about the size of a softball or bigger [and] changing shape and brightness/intensity." Others described it as a single light that floated along the tracks at a height ranging from waist to head level. One account indicated that the light was bright orange and that it floated above the ground alongside the tracks. Yet another description reported red and blue flashes of light. Most accounts seem to agree on two points: that the phenomenon appeared as a single light and that it was closely associated with the tracks.

Considering the environment in which the light appeared, there are several possible explanations. Although the tracks ran adjacent to swampland, close proximity of the light to the rails appears to rule out swamp gas. A number of the descriptions closely resemble many other railroad-associated lights, the sources of which remain unknown. A possible clue is that when rails are removed, most such lights vanish. Again, this suggests some relationship between the metal, some light-producing energy source, and the lights themselves. This hypothesis is supported by the marked if not complete decline in reported sightings during the several decades that have elapsed since the rails were removed. If sightings continued to occur for a brief period after the tracks were lifted, there is yet another possible explanation. Highway 30 crosses the former railroad at a distance of about one-half mile, and lights of southbound vehicles certainly were visible to the observer. Until vegetation growth obscured the view, probably around 1990, such sightings could have continued.

Most fascinating is the gory and heartbreaking legend associated with the Pactolus Light, which tells of one— possibly two—tragic deaths. But this legend differs from most railroad-related tales in that it did not result from a train accident. Rather, it involves cold-blooded murder. According to the story, around 1910 a young man named Edwin Cox rode his horse from Greenville to Pactolus, a distance of about nine miles. There, he planned to surprise his fiancée (or, in one version, girlfriend to whom he planned to propose) who had taken the train from her home in Richmond, Virginia, back to North Carolina where she was enrolled in East Carolina Teachers' Training School in Greenville (later East Carolina University). The train was late, darkness had fallen, and Cox was unfamiliar with the area. The legend fails to indicate whether he planned to continue waiting for the train or to return to Greenville.

At this point, the story takes a grim turn. Three locals walking along the tracks saw the horse and decided it would be easier to ride than to walk. Hiding alongside the tracks, they ambushed Edwin Cox as he rode by. He was brutally murdered, and his body was hidden in the bushes. Meanwhile, the spooked horse broke away and made its way back to Greenville several days later. Cox's body was never found. When the woman, identified only as "Glenna," finally arrived in Pactolus and learned of Cox's death, it is said that she soon died of a broken heart. The light, according to legend, is one carried by the ghost of Edwin Cox to show his lady love that, indeed, he was there to meet her.

Before the reader sheds too many tears over the incredibly sad tale of Edwin Cox and his lady friend Glenna, let's review and question some of the story's key details. Under close scrutiny, the account raises many more questions than it answers:

- ✦ According to 1910 census data, no one named Edwin Cox lived in Pitt County.
- ✦ Detailed East Carolina student records disclose that from 1909–1911 the only female student from Richmond, Virginia, was Emma Wilcox. There was no student with the first name of Glenna enrolled during those years.
- ✦ Why would Glenna have traveled on a railroad spur that passed through Pactolus en route to Washington (NC) rather than go directly to Greenville, her final destination, on the main line?
- ✦ If Cox's body was never found, there were no witnesses to the killing, and there is no reference to the miscreants being apprehended, how did so many very specific details of his death (e.g., darkness had fallen; three assailants; stealing his horse as the motive for the killing; his body dragged into the bushes) become part of the legend? And how could Glenna, upon arriving in Pactolus, have learned of his death?

⚡ How could Cox have transported himself, Glenna, and her luggage on one horse?

⚡ Unfortunately, death records were not recorded in North Carolina until 1913, so no official records of either death—if indeed they ever happened—exist.

⚡ And of greatest significance, perhaps, why, if the light is carried by the ghost of Edward Cox who supposedly was murdered in Pactolus, are all known reported sightings of strange lights from a spot more than five miles north of the supposed crime scene?

The Pactolus Light is the best-known ghost light legend in the state's East Central region. A light (or lights) of some type and of unknown source almost certainly once lured people to the Carl Morris Road rail crossing. Accounts differ in regard to whether the mysterious light still appears. Although I believe it vanished after the rails were removed and vegetation obscured the view toward Highway 30, the accompanying legend lives on as a tragic tale of enduring love.

Smithfield (Johnston County): Mill Creek Bridge (bridge)

(*Note*: Although Smithfield is located in the Central region, Mill Creek is south of the city and east of I-95.) Smithfield is at the intersection of I-95 and US Highway 70B about twenty-four miles southeast of Raleigh. Mill Creek is fourteen miles south of Smithfield on US 701. The specific location of the Mill Creek Bridge is unknown. Today, several roads and bridges cross the creek south of the community.

The ghostly lights that supposedly appeared on Mill Creek Bridge present a classic example of the frustrating challenges confronted when one attempts to conduct this type of research. Let's begin our search with the most detailed description of the light:

Spectral lights danced on Mill Creek Bridge in the 1950s. Old timers in the area say the *luminescent flashes* [emphasis mine] are the ghost of an old black man being lashed by his cruel master. In May 1820, Master Lynch and one of his slaves, Old Squire, were clearing land near the wooden bridge here. Lynch lashed at the slave with his whip one too many times, and the large black man struck back at his master with a hoe. Old Squire buried Lynch under the bridge, and before long, people started noticing strange things at the wooden crossing. Lanterns would go out as the bridge was crossed, and weird sounds emanated from under it. Once, a man's cane was snatched from his hand as he stepped onto the bridge, only to be returned to him when he reached the other side. Old Squire confessed to the murder on his death bed.

After reading the foregoing passage, does anything stand out as being a bit strange to you? For example, where was the bridge located? Or, in a seemingly egregious oversight, where is a reference to the source of the lengthy quote? Certainly, it should seem strange to the reader for a passage of this length to appear without a source being cited (see citations in references for this chapter). Actually, what appears above is copied almost verbatim from several of the references cited.

The tale seems to have first appeared in Nancy Roberts's 1959 book, published 139 years after the supposed killing occurred. Are we to believe that the story remained dormant for that length of time and suddenly (re)emerged? This seems extremely unlikely. In the prologue to the book, Roberts does indicate that the "Thing at the Bridge" story was told to her by a Smithfield resident, H. V. Rose, an amateur historian who was interested in local lore. Where he heard the story is unknown, and Rose, who died in the late 1950s, took his source of information to the grave.

As you know, I have identified fifty-four ghost lights and/or legends in the state. Yet one of the major references to supernatural phenomena, Dennis William Hauck's *Haunted Places: The National Directory,* includes the Mill Creek Bridge Light as one of only four ghost lights in North Carolina, which places it on par with the famous Brown Mountain and Maco Lights. Hauck cites Roberts as his source of information. Dale Kaczmarek also includes Mill Creek as one of only fifteen North Carolina spook lights. He copied Hauck word-for-word (but did cite his source). As indicated above, the details contained in each of the three listed sources are basically identical to those found in Hauck's and Kaczmarek's accounts. Not one of the websites provides its source of information. So we are left with five accounts of events that supposedly occurred 139 years before being told by a local historian and, I'm sure, a creator and teller of tall tales.

And what about those "spectral lights" supposedly seen dancing on Mill Creek Bridge during the "1950s," the date that appears in all but Roberts's initial account? A passage from her book offers an interesting clue to the origin of that date: "During the Fifties it was a common sight at night to see a light bobbing up and down around the bridge. And those who saw it would say, 'See, there is Lynch lashing Old Squire now to his heart's content.'" I believe Hauk incorrectly interpreted the reference to the "Fifties" to mean the 1950s, rather than the almost-certain 1850s. This hypothesis is supported by the fact that I have not found anyone in the area who has a clue about the Mill Creek Bridge or the accompanying legend (other than what they might have read).

Williamston (Martin County):
Screaming Bridge (swamp)

(*Note*: Although Williamston is in the northeast region, the nearby light is some distance south of US 64.) Site is believed to be approximately seven miles east of Bear Grass. Easiest access is to take NC 171 south from Jamesville (US 64) for seven miles to Holly Springs Church Road (about one-half mile north of Roberson Store or one mile north of Farmlife), which branches off 171 to the northwest. Take this road two miles to Yarrell Creek Road and turn left. Exact location of the Screaming Bridge is unknown.

Martin County's Screaming Bridge legend is within a common folklore genre. It is but one of perhaps a half dozen such tales of tragic events—usually an automobile accident—associated with a bridge that are told in various locations around the country. As urban legends, all bridge-related stories have basically the same theme: some horrible event resulted in the death of one or more people, whose ghosts still haunt the area with anguished, spine-tingling screams. At some of the sites, including Yarrell Creek Road, strange lights also supposedly appear.

Few North Carolina ghost stories can match Screaming Bridge in number of imaginative explanations. One tale tells of a young girl from the Yarrell family who, when seated on a stump, lost her balance, fell into Sweetwater Creek, and drowned at a spot beneath a wooden bridge that was replaced long ago. Her ghost (a light image) appears on occasion, and her blood-curdling screams pierce the dark night. (A hardened skeptic might ask, "Why are screams not heard during the daytime, as well?")

Another version tells of a woman wearing a cat costume and red contact lenses who had attended a Halloween party. After the party, she picked up her baby and was headed home when she was distracted (tuning the radio according to one account; a contemporary version, no doubt, would have her texting) and drove off the bridge. Both she and her baby drowned. Some sources tell of flashes of light, whereas others indicate seeing eerie red lights, supposedly from her red contacts.

Perhaps the goriest twist to the legend tells of a Mrs. Yarrell who, after being beaten by her husband, hanged herself at the bridge. Her sister found the body, became distraught, and committed suicide by slitting her throat (or wrists in one version). The blood stain reportedly still appears on occasion, and glowing eyes still shine menacingly on some dark nights.

Although lights take second place to sounds in this legend, the origin story is interesting and quite relevant in the context of folklore. It illustrates the way in which, through time, different stories evolve as variants to a central motif—in this case, various scenarios that supposedly explain blood-curdling screams and sinister lights. In the case of this Screaming Bridge, several interesting facts stand out. Two of the legends relate to Yarrell family members who lived in the area during the mid-1800s. The third tells of a woman wearing contact lenses who drove off the bridge and died. Inasmuch as contact lenses did not become widely used until the 1960s, this places the events at least a century apart. Here, we have a case of enduring screams and lights, but widely varied and temporally spaced legends. And as is true of so many purported ghost lights, today no one in the area seems to be aware of any tragic event or associated ghostly phenomena having occurred anyplace along Yarrell Creek Road.

Chapter Four

SOUTHEAST

⚡ ⚡ ⚡

MOST VISITORS TO North Carolina's southeastern region are drawn by the attraction of its sandy beaches and tasty seafood, or by the amenities of the area's largest city, Wilmington. But those who leave the coast and wander inland on the area's back roads will be treated to an entirely different world. Here, the numerous small communities and rural landscapes encapsulate both the problems and cautious optimism evident throughout much of today's rural South. It is an area where the palimpsest of a bygone era often bleeds through the contemporary landscape, offering a sharp visible contrast between a rustic past and contemporary social and economic realities. As is true for much of eastern North Carolina, earliest European settlement occurred during the first half of the eighteenth century. Tobacco and peanuts formed the basis of a once-thriving agricultural economy. But perhaps more so than anywhere else in the state, economic decline and rural and small-town depopulation have taken a visible toll on the region. Away from Wilmington and the coast, much of the area lags behind other parts of the state in most economic indices.

In terms of ghost lights, however, the Southeast leads the state in a number of categories. First, no other area can match its rich tradition of lights and their accompanying legends. Second, all ten of the documented lights almost certainly appeared at one time, and six may still appear today. Third, seven of the lights appear, or once appeared, in association with railroad tracks. Unfortunately, several of them vanished when the rails were removed. Once again, this suggests the existence of some as yet unidentified relationship between rails and the unexplained ghost lights with which they are (or in some instances were) associated. Fourth, for more than a century the region boasted what many ghost light buffs considered to be the country's most famous light, the mysterious glowing orb that for more than a century hovered over the tracks near Maco Station. Finally, the region appears to be home to the popular legend motif of a railroad-related ghost light being the lantern carried by a revenant in search of his head, which was lost in a tragic train accident and never found. Since the 1800s, thousands of thrill seekers and just plain curious folks have been drawn to remote spots throughout the area in the hope of seeing a ghostly illumination pierce the darkness. With a bit of luck, you can, too.

TABLE 4. Southeast NC Ghost Lights

Community	County	Light	Environment
Bolivia	Brunswick	Half Hell	Roadway
Clarkton	Bladen	Buie	Railroad
Evergreen	Columbus	Evergreen	Railroad
Fair Bluff	Columbus	Causey's Road	Railroad
Maco	Brunswick	Maco	Railroad (tracks removed)
Mintz	Sampson	Mintz	Railroad (tracks removed)
Stedman	Cumberland	No known name	Railroad
Vander	Cumberland	Vander	Railroad
Whiteville	Columbus	Old Tram Road	Roadway
Wilmington	New Hanover	Mt. Misery Road	Roadway

Bolivia (Brunswick County): Half Hell Lights (roadway)

Bolivia is located on US Highway 17 about twenty miles southeast of Wilmington. Just over a mile southeast of the small community, Midway Road branches off in a south-easterly direction. The settlement of Half Hell is on Midway Road, approximately one mile from the main highway. Midway Road continues southward, eventually intersecting with NC 211 at Smith settlement. Sources do not mention a specific location along the road at which a light supposedly appears.

A number of people have reported seeing strange lights while traveling Midway Road a few miles south of Bolivia. One informant, identified only as "Tamara" on her web page, explained a light reported by "Astra," as follows: "What your family witnessed was indeed a ghost around here, it's called Half Hell Lights, [sic] people describe seeing lights that chase

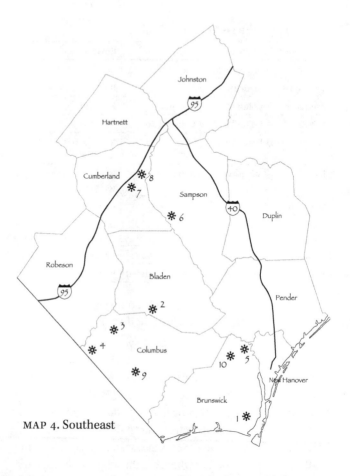

MAP 4. Southeast

their car or sometimes come through the car. It's been going on for quite a while." Several others report having seen a light that follows vehicles before it gradually dims and finally vanishes.

Although I have not traveled Midway Road at night, one possible source of the "mystery" light is quite apparent. From the point the road branches off US 17 to where it intersects with NC 211 is about six miles. Over this relatively short distance, nearly two dozen rural streets and other roads join Midway Road. This suggests that lights of distant vehicles may appear ahead of or behind an observer for a short period of time and then vanish as the vehicle turns off Midway Road onto one of the many branching arteries. Light or no light, a trip to this location is worth the effort if for no other reason than you can boast that you've "been to (Half) Hell and back!"

Clarkton (Bladen County):
Buie [Bowie; Buoy] Light (railroad)

Three miles southeast of Clarkton on NC Highway 211, Elkton Road branches off to the north. In a very short distance, the road crosses the CSX railroad tracks. A light reportedly appears occasionally when one looks down the tracks in a westerly direction toward Clarkton.

As is true of most such phenomena, the Buie Light is a bit difficult to pin down. The various information sources are not much help. There are several descriptions by people who claim to have seen a light when looking down the tracks. They seem to agree, however, on only two points: the light is best viewed during a light rain and the vantage point for sighting is looking westward down the CSX tracks at the point they are crossed by Elkton Road. Unfortunately, reports of what is seen vary greatly. (Several of the sources suggest parking on the track while watching for the light. As it is still in use, this is not recommended!)

Much information on the Buie Light comes from a single (now defunct) source, "The Haunted Light at Clarkton" by Daniel T. Edwards. He describes a yellow-orange glow about the size of a lit cigar that floated above the tracks at an estimated distance of a quarter mile. It was visible for a couple minutes before flickering out. It then reappeared for about fifteen seconds before vanishing again. Another anonymous witness saw the light appear near a trestle, swing back and forth across the tracks, and then fly away over the trees. On one occasion, the light reportedly followed the rails and came all the way up to the viewer.

While researching the Buie Light, I communicated with several area residents, none of whom claimed to have ever seen or heard of anything unusual. I do believe, however, that *something* appears, at least on occasion, when one looks down the rails toward Clarkton. Specifically what it might be remains a mystery. Several roads closely parallel the tracks, and it is possible that the lights are those of vehicles. So, too, the reported lights could be from vehicles crossing the tracks on US 701 in Clarkton. Many lights of unknown origin do appear in conjunction with rails, such as those that appear regularly between Ahoskie and Aulander (chapter 2) and the Maco and Mintz Lights (this chapter), both of which vanished when the rails were removed.

It is interesting that any reference to a legend accompanying the Buie Light is rather vague. Edwards indicated that a railroad man was killed, "but how we are not sure. . . . It is said to [have happened] sometime around the turn of the [twentieth] century." No further details of this fatality seem to exist, and Edwards did not reveal his source of information. Another source indicates that, "We do know a man by the name of Buie was . . . killed." But, again, there are no details. Strangely, only a single reference suggests that the light is that of a lantern carried by a decapitated railroad man now searching for his lost head.

Commenting on his sighting, Edwards stated, "It was so sad. The light seemed to be a man's doomed soul perhaps, searching for the truth, or maybe his head. I do not know. I am certain, however, of what I saw, and the melancholy of the whole event." If you happen to be in the Clarkton area on a rainy night, you might want to go to the Elkton crossing and look toward the community to see if Buie's doomed soul is still searching for his lost head—or perhaps for the truth, whatever it may be. But don't park on the tracks, or you, too, may become a source of local legend!

Evergreen (Columbus County):
Evergreen Light (railroad)

Evergreen is a small settlement located on NC 242 one mile north of the junction of US 74 and NC 130. Location of the reported light is unknown.

The only information I have found on the Evergreen Light is from the *Ghosts of America* website, where three anonymous entries provide few useful details. The two that claimed eyewitness accounts are both extremely vague. Neither mentions what, specifically, the viewers saw, or where and when the sightings occurred. One description indicates that the writer "heard of [*sic*] some people talk about the Evergreen Light," and went to check it out one night. Unfortunately, there are no details indicating when or where the search occurred, or whether a light was seen. Four other witnesses, however, reported seeing "orbs of light bouncing around everywhere." Another report indicates that many people witnessed the light over a period of years. Unfortunately, this account also fails to mention the light's physical appearance, the location where it supposedly appeared, or the time span during which it was seen. The contributor claims to have seen a light that hovered for some time in a ditch before it flew over the trees and vanished.

One account indicates that during the 1940s (and presumably before) a railroad passed through the area. It states that a truck carrying twelve youngsters and two adults from a church service was struck by a train, resulting in the death of all fourteen passengers. Unfortunately, there is no mention of a date, and I am unable to find any reference to such an accident. But where there was (or is) a light, there seemingly must be an accompanying explanatory legend. Evidently the light, if it ever existed, vanished some years ago after the area in which it supposedly was seen was drained and converted to farmland. Based on several local inquiries, memories of the Evergreen Ghost Light have flickered out as has the light itself.

Fair Bluff (Columbus County): Causey's Road Light (railroad)

Fair Bluff is located at the intersection of US 76 and NC 904, approximately three miles from the South Carolina border. A light of unknown origin reportedly appeared when a viewer looked northward along the tracks from any of the roads that cross the railroad south of town (including several roads just across the border in South Carolina).

The Fair Bluff Light is one of those spooky enigmas that is difficult, if not impossible, to pin down. As is true of most reported ghost lights, there are individuals who swear to have seen the Flair Bluff Light, and some of them claim to have seen them on numerous occasions. Unfortunately, specific details about the sightings are usually extremely vague or entirely lacking. In the case of Fair Bluff, a substantial number of area residents indicate that they have never seen a light themselves but have heard that [fill in the blank] once saw it. Finally, several local residents are convinced that it is nothing more than a local myth. Having visited the site myself, I am quite sure that lights occasionally were visible to someone looking northward along the tracks of the now abandoned railroad. Whether they were "ghost" lights, however, is another matter, as I shall attempt to explain.

Most eyewitness accounts appear in *Ghosts of America*, "Fair Bluff, North Carolina Ghost Sightings." They describe a single light that was seen briefly at a distance and then vanished abruptly. One viewer indicated that "there was never a sound and it always seemed to disappear suddenly." Another described a light that "suddenly . . . appear[ed] and kept getting closer then disappeared." One description stands out from the others in that a "distant glow," rather than a bright light, was seen.

Each of the foregoing makes sense when one considers the relationship between the railroad right-of-way and local roads. Causey Road closely parallels the (now abandoned) railroad. All reported sightings occurred from locations at which a road branching off Causey crossed the tracks. Two sites in particular stand out: looking northward along the tracks from Rough Fork Road, or from Deadridge Road crossing. From either location, lights of vehicles would have been visible as they cross the tracks on any of the several roads between the vantage point and Fair Bluff. The described "distant glow" is a common occurrence under conditions when lights of a nearby approaching vehicle cannot be seen directly. This would occur when a vehicle traveling southward on Causey Road turned off onto one of the side roads before reaching the viewer.

The tracks have been abandoned for some time now, and the right-of-way is densely overgrown. Because of the vegetation, it is not possible to see the lights of vehicles (other, perhaps, than a distant glow) crossing or traveling on Causey Road.

There remains yet another possibility. As you now know, some relationship exists between rails and certain ghost lights. Although its nature remains a mystery, it is entirely possible that at one time an eerie light of unknown origin did, indeed, hover over the tracks that parallel Causey Road.

The Fair Bluff Light is unique in one very significant way. To my knowledge, there is no legend associated with the phenomenon. This, in itself, suggests that the light may not have existed, at least as an unexplained anomaly. Hilda Small, who works at the Fair Bluff Depot Museum, came to the community in 1958. She claims never to have seen the light and knows little about it. She mentioned a friend who lived along Causey Road all of his seventy-four years and never saw the light. Regarding the mystery, her response to my inquiry fairly well sums it up: "I wish I could be more helpful—but no one can give us positive proof. . . . So you see, some folks had big imaginations."

Maco (Brunswick County):
Maco Light [Joe Baldwin Light]
(railroad—tracks removed)

Maco is a small rural settlement on the former Atlantic Coast Line (now CSX) Railroad and US Highways 74 and 76, about twelve miles west of Wilmington.

By any measure, the light that appeared for at least 110 years in the vicinity of Maco Station (more correctly, a rail siding) was one of North Carolina's—and the nation's—most fascinating, enigmatic, and reliable ghost lights. And it is very likely that its accompanying legend may play a significant role in ghost light–related folklore. Thousands of people were thrilled (and often spooked) by the light, which rarely disappointed viewers with its amazing, unexplained, luminous display. The light even inspired the lyrics of several folksongs and was featured in a number of national magazines. To add to the lore, it may be the only ghost light in the country reportedly seen and asked about by a president. Passing through the area by rail, President Grover Cleveland is said to have seen a strange light and asked about the glowing orb.

According to most accounts, the light first appeared in 1867 and vanished when the tracks were removed in 1977. It was my good fortune to see the eerily glowing orb in the early 1960s. As a member of the East Carolina University geography faculty, I took several students on a field trip to the Wilmington area. One of them suggested that we go to see the famous Maco Ghost Light. At the time, I had never heard of ghost lights by that or any other name. But always ready for a new adventure, I replied "Sure!" and off we went. What we saw was absolutely astounding. After several minutes of suspecting that we were on a proverbial wild goose chase, a strangely glowing pale white orb, about the size of a basketball, appeared floating several feet above the tracks. Rather than a direct illumination, it looked like light passing through fog or smoke. Needless to say, this initial sighting instilled in me an interest in ghost lights that now spans more than a half century.

As is true of most ghost lights, a plethora of fiction and a paucity of verifiable fact surround the Maco Light. Nonetheless, one thing is certain: there was a light. Unfortunately, what evolved through time is an abundance of lore, very little of which withstands close scrutiny. According to most versions of the legend, the nature and sequence of events occurred as described in the following passages.

As the story goes, a strange light first appeared over the tracks of the Wilmington, Manchester, and Augusta Railroad in 1867 (or, according to different versions, in 1862 or 1873). All accounts agree, however, that it was visible near Hood's Creek, located a short distance east of the small rural settlement of Farmer's Turnout, which was renamed Maco in 1890. Descriptions of the light vary considerably. The earliest known account describes two lights, one white and another green, weaving back-and-forth about three feet above the tracks. Most witnesses, however, reported seeing but a single white light, although there are reports that the light changed from white to green, or from white to green to red. In terms of luminescence, descriptions vary from appearing like the dim light of a 25-watt bulb to a light bright enough to cast a shadow and read by.

Nearly everyone agrees that the light appeared above the rails at a height of several feet. Some viewers claim other motions, particularly swinging back and forth as would a lantern carried by a railroad worker. A few witnesses claim the light veered away from the tracks, soared over the heads of viewers, and flew off into the woods before it vanished. In my experience, the light remained at a constant height of several feet and directly above the rails. When approached, the light receded; when I backed away, the light followed, though always remaining over the tracks. This movement, of course, made the experience even more inexplicable and spooky! Based on what our group saw, I tend to agree with John Harden, who stated, "The Maco [L]ight never varies a fraction from a given course. . . . It always appear[ed] about three feet above the left rail, [when] facing east—always."

In terms of sightings, the light appeared throughout the year, and, according to most reports, its appearance was not affected by weather conditions, including rain or fog. As is true of all lights, it appeared brighter on dark nights than under conditions of bright moonlight. Before it vanished permanently in 1977, the light did disappear for brief periods. For example, after the 1886 Charleston, South Carolina, earthquake, the light inexplicably vanished for about a month. Prior to that time, some accounts indicate that two lights were seen; after the quake, only a single light appeared. Why the light disappeared following a seismic event remains a baffling mystery, as does its reappearance as a single, rather than dual, luminous object.

Whereas thousands of people witnessed the strange glow of the Maco Light, no one was more famous than President Grover Cleveland who, according to historical accounts, either saw or heard of the light in October of 1889 (or 1879, or 1894). The tales of his sighting serve as an excellent introduction to the disparate legends that surround the Maco Light. Cleveland was not president in 1879, so that date can be ruled out. Actually, the date makes little difference; in both 1889 and 1894, he was in office. It is his sighting and the various circumstances under which he supposedly witnessed the phenomenon that are of greatest interest. Evidently, his sighting was reported to the press, and the widespread media coverage suddenly catapulted the Maco Station ghost light into national, if not international, prominence.

In one account, Cleveland was riding in his presidential Pullman when he saw a mysterious glow flickering in the woods to the right of his railcar. Of course, this version of the sighting does not coincide with most descriptions that place the light directly over the rails. He asked the conductor what he had seen and was told that it was the "Maco Station Light" (the veracity of this statement is in doubt, simply because the station was not named "Maco" until 1890).

In another version, when the train pulled into the siding, the president got out of his Pullman to stretch his legs by walking along the tracks. He noticed the brakeman carrying both a red and a green lantern, which he thought was strange. Upon asking the brakeman why he carried two lanterns, the president was told of the Maco Light. Because of the confusion it caused to passing trains, the two lanterns of different colors were used to distinguish between the railroad lights and the single white Maco Light—reportedly carried by a "ghost along these tracks that waves a lantern." In this version, the president evidently did not actually see the light. The account continues to state that he was then told the story of Joe Baldwin who, as the tale goes, lost his head in a horrible accident while heroically attempting to prevent a crash one night in 1867. Like so many ghost light legends, however, the Joe Baldwin tale appears to be just that, an imaginative—yet baseless—myth.

According to the legend, Joe Baldwin was a conductor who worked for the Wilmington, Manchester, and Augusta Railroad (which later became the Atlantic Coast Line). Joe, as the story goes, was married and lived in Wilmington. One dark and rainy night in 1867 (by most accounts), Joe suddenly realized that the train's last car, the one in which he was riding, was slowing down. Somehow, it had become disconnected from the other cars. He also knew that another train was following closely behind and if he didn't act immediately, a horrible crash was just minutes away. In a panic, he grabbed his lantern and ran to the platform at the back of his car to signal the engineer of the onrushing train. His frantic signaling, made by waving his lantern back and forth, went unheeded, however, resulting in a deadly—although historically undocumented—crash.

In the accident, as the tale goes, Joe Baldwin was decapitated, and his severed head was never found. Soon thereafter, what came to be known as the Maco (or Joe Baldwin) Light began to appear. Baldwin, who supposedly gave his life in an attempt to save his train, spent the next 110 years searching for his lost head. In this version, his futile search ended, and the light from his lantern was finally extinguished when the tracks were removed in 1977.

Historically, the Maco Light is quite significant. It appears to be the very first reference in the United States to a light attributed to the revenant of a decapitated railroad employee carrying a lantern in an eternal search for his lost head. If this is true, and I believe it is, the legend began in 1867 (according to most accounts) and spread from the Maco area to more than fifteen other sites in North Carolina alone. It is far and away the dominant legend motif in North Carolina's ghostly railroad-related folklore.

But now the Joe Baldwin legend takes a very strange twist, truly one that lends credence to the old adage that "truth is stranger than fiction." What follows is the result of meticulous research conducted by geographer James C. Burke, who in 2004 was a graduate student at the University of North Carolina at Greensboro. In conjunction with a larger research project on the history of early railroads in North Carolina, Burke included a detailed study of the Maco/Joe Baldwin Light legend. To his surprise, there was no public record of any kind that listed a Joe or Joseph Baldwin living in or near Wilmington. And no record exists of a Baldwin having been employed by the Wilmington, Manchester, and Augusta Railroad. Further, the railroad's schedule did not match the two trains in a close proximity scenario as presented in the legend. In fact, there is no record of a major crash in the area during 1867.

Burke did find newspaper accounts of a crash close to Farmer's Turnout (later Maco) in January 1856, eleven years before the crash on which the Baldwin legend is based. And amazingly, records show that a railroad employee named Charles Baldwin was injured and died of his injuries several days after the accident. Here, however, the story takes an unexpected turn. You will recall that, according to legend, Joe Baldwin died a hero, as he desperately tried to stop an onrushing train. In the well-documented 1856 crash, it was the train's engine, not the rear car, that was disconnected. The engineer ran the engine ahead in an attempt to fix some defective pumps. When he backed the engine to return and couple with the cars, conductor Charles Baldwin did not signal the location of the rest of the train. The engineer, returning at a high rate of speed, collided with the stationary cars, which resulted in serious damage to several of them. The accident also resulted in injury to and the ultimate death of Charles Baldwin. So rather than being a hero, Charles Baldwin's inattention to a very important responsibility was the primary cause of the crash. How Charles Baldwin and an accident in 1856 due to his negligence morphed into a heroic Joe Baldwin and a crash in 1867 remains a mystery. Strangely, there is no record of a ghost light in the area until after the undocumented 1867 crash.

All of the many serious attempts to explain the Maco Light, including those by various scientific research teams, ended in frustrating failure. What is known is that a light of unknown origin was visible on a fairly regular basis for more than a century. It also vanished when the tracks were removed, which suggests some relationship between the metal rails and the light that hovered above them. What that relationship might have been remains a nagging mystery. Automobile lights can be discounted because the light appeared long before cars existed. And, on at least one occasion, all lights within a considerable area were turned off, and the ghost light continued to shine. Based on my own observation, the light could not have been caused by such commonly suggested agents as swamp gas, phosphorescent swamp vapors, earthquake lights, or foxfire. Everyone loves a mystery. Perhaps it is best that what once was one of the nation's most famous ghost lights remains an eternal enigma.

Mintz (Sampson County):
Mintz Light (railroad—tracks removed)

Although several locations are suggested, the precise spot where the Mintz Light once appeared is unknown. Reportedly, it was seen somewhere in the vicinity of Mintz, a tiny settlement located on NC Highway 411 between Roseboro and Garland.

The Mintz and Maco Lights share much in common. According to most accounts, their appearance was similar. At both locations, most descriptions are of a white light that floated a few feet above railroad tracks. The Mintz Light is variously described as resembling the light of an approaching train or a small light that swung back and forth above the tracks, appearing like someone carrying a lantern. Yet another description is of a glow that hovered over the tracks, bounced, and vanished. This account, at least in terms of a glow that hovered over the tracks, is an identical match to most descriptions of the Maco Light. And, as happened in Maco, the light vanished when the tracks through Mintz were removed in 1980.

The Mintz and Maco lights also share the same common railroad decapitation legend. There are, however, several different versions of the Mintz tale. In one account, a deaf man carrying a lantern was walking along the tracks on a very dark night. Upon sighting the man on the tracks, the engineer of an approaching train sounded a warning whistle, which, of course, the man was unable to hear. When hit by the engine, his head was severed and never located. For decades, his lantern-carrying ghost walked the tracks nightly in search of his lost skull. In a different version, a track watchman fell into the path of a speeding train and was decapitated. Neither the body nor the head were ever found (which, of course, makes verification rather difficult!). In yet another twist, after the watchman was beheaded, his headless body picked up the lantern and vanished. This legend fails to indicate how or whether the lantern returned to glow in the darkness of night.

As so often is the case, the only reliable historical data pertaining to the light is that it disappeared in 1980, immediately after the tracks were lifted. I found no references to railroad-related deaths in the area, and no one with whom I communicated was aware of the legend's origin in regard to either the supposed event or date it occurred. Evidently, the light was seen for many years and, according to local residents, was a popular nightly tourist attraction during the 1950s and 1960s. In this context, it is significant to note that the period between the end of World War II and the introduction and spread of television as a form of entertainment during the 1960s was the peak of ghost light interest and viewing.

Swamp gas and car lights are the only suggested sources. Swamp gas can be ruled out simply because of the light's regular appearance, its close (rather than random) proximity to the railroad tracks, and the fact that it did not appear again after the rails were removed. Without having seen the light myself, or the location of the tracks relative to various area roadways, I cannot assess the possible role of vehicle lights.

There is, of course, the legend (if you believe in revenants carrying lanterns to illuminate their headless search). But it seems that something much more significant is involved here. Mintz and Maco are two of several locations where lights vanished when tracks were removed. It seems very probable that some as yet unidentified force—perhaps a rail-related electrical field, ambient light reflected from the polished rails, or some other unknown agent—was at work.

Stedman (Cumberland County):
Stedman Light (railroad)

Stedman is located on NC Highway 24, between Vander and Autryville. No details exist of a specific location. (It may, in fact, be a reference to the Vander Light, which is located between the two communities.)

I found but a single reference to a strange light reportedly seen from Stedman. A person identified only as Dulles and of unknown age indicated that, when he was young, elders would tell youngsters never to go to the railroad tracks at night. They were told the now familiar railroad decapitation legend, including the lore of the resulting revenant wandering the tracks with a lantern in search of his lost head.

The tracks that passed through Stedman were removed in the late 1980s, and no one with whom I communicated seems to recall the grizzly tale. It is possible, if not probable, that the story of the light is simply a local adaptation of the well-known and quite active Vander Light. This eerie illumination was seen for decades from a vantage point located on the tracks just east of Vander and about five miles west of Stedman.

Vander (Cumberland County):
Vander Light (railroad)

Vander is about 3.5 miles southeast of Fayetteville at the intersection of Clinton, John B. Carter, and Sunnyside School Roads. Most sources indicate that the lights appear when looking eastward along the tracks from the point where Old Vander Road crosses the CSX railroad just east of the community.

When one looks eastward down the CSX railroad tracks from the Old Vander Road crossing, *something* glows in the distance. It appears repeatedly and is visible throughout the night, although most frequently during the early evening and only sporadically after midnight. As so often is the case, descriptions of the Vander Light are so varied that it is impossible to know whether what I saw was the light that is reported by others, or something entirely different.

One viewer saw what he described as a faint glowing light moving from side to side. This coincides with what I saw—a rather large, yet very faint glow above the distant horizon that always moved from left to right (north to south) for a short distance. At the time I assumed that the glow was from the headlights of cars traveling westward on Clinton Road (NC 24). At a distance of about two miles, there is a slight bend in the road that allows headlights to shine very briefly

Vander Light viewing spot

toward the viewing site. Additionally, the time it takes vehicles to travel that stretch of road coincides with the duration of the light's appearance. This theory is supported by
the observations of others who indicate that the light is difficult, if not impossible, to pinpoint in terms of its distant location. Also, the frequency of vehicles traveling west on Clinton
Road would be greatest in the early evening and diminish
after midnight.

Other descriptions are of a light that resembles a lantern
(you guessed it!) swinging back and forth above the tracks.
One of the more interesting accounts is of a light that shines
in the middle of the tracks, is constantly visible, and can
be seen at any hour of the night. This suggests a stationary
light in the distance, something I have not witnessed and

for which I find no evidence or possible source. Another account describes a light that rises and grows dim, then briefly brightens as it falls back before dimming again into a soft glow and disappearing. This description somewhat coincides with what I saw, and it supports the car light theory.

Several viewers report a light that moves toward or away from them along the tracks. In an apparent anomaly, one observer claimed that the closer he got to the light, the faster the light moved toward him. This is directly opposite of the movement of the Maco Light that backed away as one moved toward it on the rails. A single account reports a light that comes out of the woods and travels down the tracks; if one approaches the light, it vanishes, only to reappear behind the viewer. As so often is the case, different people see and report different things, thereby making it impossible to describe the actual illumination with any certainty. Of course, in many locations (such as Early Station, described in chapter 2), lights do appear in a variety of shapes, colors, and movements. It is possible that a similar situation existed—or may still exist—here.

Certain aspects of the Vander Light remain in doubt. For example, conditions under which the light appears are in question. Some insist that it is visible nightly and at all hours. Others say it only appears on dark and moonless nights. When it first appeared also is in question. Several accounts indicate that it was first seen in the early 1700s, long before railroads or automobiles. Yet there is no mention of a ghost light in the area in the WPA book on North Carolina published in 1939 or, for that matter, any other early reference of which I am aware. Several writers indicate that the light first appeared only "recently" or a "short time ago." One source gave an approximate date—in or about 1978.

And, as the numerous descriptions of a light resembling a lantern that swings back and forth suggest, we have yet another legend involving an accident that resulted in a decapitation and lost head. Here, however, the story becomes vague. In one account, an unidentified passenger left his seat to smoke. The train abruptly stopped, resulting in his falling off and being beheaded (very unlikely, since trains do not stop instantly when braking). A different version (and similar to the legend behind the Maco Light) tells of an accident "quite a few years ago." A man in the caboose saw a train rapidly approaching from the rear. He grabbed his lantern and began frantically swinging it back and forth to signal the engineer who, evidently, failed to see the lantern. The flagman was killed in the crash, and his head was never found. This account closely parallels the Joe Baldwin story. As is almost universally true of railroad-related legends, there is no date for or account of the alleged accident, and no mention is made of the deceased's name. We must remember that nearly always, this is the stuff of folk legends rather than of reality.

A number of scientists have studied the Vander Light and suggested several theories in their attempts to explain the phenomenon. One researcher suggested that it is the flame of a phosphorous compound such as phosphine. There is marshland in the area, but neither the descriptions nor frequency of appearance support a swamp gas theory. Another expert believes the light could be an electrostatic discharge from the rails. I believe that what I saw was the glow from the indirect light of distant vehicles. But with so many varied descriptions, who knows? Perhaps Dale Kaczmarek got it right in suggesting that the light "could be nothing more than a nocturnal reflection . . . of [people] only imagining things." On the other hand, Harold Black, writing in the *News and*

Observer (1961), suggested (jokingly, I trust) that the lights are associated with the horde of flying saucers that crashed to create the Carolina bays, and they are "nothing but a flying Saucerian looking for his long lost disintegrator ray gun." At least this is an imaginative and refreshing departure from the folktale of an endless search for a severed head.

Whiteville (Columbus County): Old Tram Road Light (roadway)

Old Tram Road is located approximately seven miles south of Whiteville, between highways US 701 and NC 905. It extends from White Crossing to Pole Bridge Crossing.

The Old Tram Road Light presents some interesting and rather frustrating challenges that, once again, highlight some of the problems that confront the ghost light researcher. First, the several known descriptions of the light are verbatim. They read: "On Old Tram Road—while traveling this road [I have] seen what appeared to be taillights in the distance. They would disappear and headlights would show up. The car was translucent and no driver was present. The ghost car will chase you to the end of the road, where a church stands and the light just disappears."

Unfortunately, no names are mentioned, no dates are given, and all accounts appear to have originated from a single unidentified source. Further adding to the confusion are two anonymous comments gleaned from a long-vanished website. One person indicated that "I live on [O]ld [T]ram [R]oad, and I have yet to see this . . . in my many times of coming down this road, all night and day times, I haven't seen anything remotely like this." Another nameless individual stated, "I . . . have been down [O]ld [T]ram plenty of times and have yet to see the light. . . . I'm still waiting to see it for myself."

Several written inquiries to local officials went unanswered. Perhaps the recipients either thought I was crazy for asking about a ghost light or they had no information to offer. The description does, however, provide one possibly significant clue to what is seen. Old Tram Road, now paved, passes through a five-mile patchwork of woodland and farmland. There are a number of residences, and nearly a dozen roads branch off from Old Tram. It is not only possible, but highly probable, that lights of distant vehicles, traveling in either direction, could be interpreted as being ghost lights as seen at a distance on the long and perfectly straight stretch of road. This is particularly true if they appeared and then suddenly vanished as the vehicle turned off the main road or, conversely, turned on to the road from a side street. Those who claimed not to have seen the lights were local residents who, in all probability, recognized them for what they no doubt were—vehicle lights seen at a distance.

Wilmington (New Hanover County): Mt. Misery Road (roadway)

Mt. Misery Road extends from Leland, a small settlement located approximately five miles west of Wilmington and just north of the Andrew Jackson Highway, to the vicinity of Maco and Sandy Creek on US Highways 74 and 76. The road itself is about ten miles in length and lies entirely in Brunswick County.

No one seems to know the origin of the heartrending tale of Mt. Misery Road. In fact, the legend seems to have faded from memory. The story related here is based on the only two very brief and anonymous accounts that I found. During the slave era, captive Africans were unloaded from slave ships in Wilmington, and many of them were marched the ninety-some miles to the slave market in Fayetteville. The route traveled gained the name Mt. Misery Road because of the horrible toll of human life along the way. According to accounts, those who were ill or unable to keep pace were simply killed, and their bodies were left along the roadside. Others died of illnesses, snake bites, or other causes. Supposedly, it is their restless souls that reportedly are seen or heard, or their presences otherwise felt, by people traversing Mt. Misery Road today. It also is said that lights of unknown origin occasionally appear in the woods bordering the road.

Whether ghosts or restless souls, swamp gas, the lights of vehicles traveling the area's numerous roads, or something else, the legacy of a tragic bygone era is etched into the Mt. Misery Road ghost light legend.

Chapter Five

CENTRAL

⚡ ⚡ ⚡

CENTRAL NORTH CAROLINA, the area located from border-to-border and between I-77 and I-95, is mainly piedmont country. Here, the relatively flat terrain of the Coastal Plain gives way to a staircase of gently rolling piedmont landscapes that gradually rises to merge with mountains in the west. It is also the state's heartland in terms of population, economic development, cultural activity, and social diversity. Here, the cities of Charlotte, Winston-Salem, and Raleigh flourish at the periphery of the North Carolina Research Triangle formed by Chapel Hill (University of North Carolina), Durham (Duke University), and Raleigh (North Carolina State University). It is one of the nation's most rapidly growing, prosperous, and innovative areas.

Outside of the bustling urban areas, however, the scattered small communities and rural settlements differ little from those throughout the rest of the state. It is here that we find a rich heritage of luminous legends, but, inexplicably, of the eight lights within the region for which documentation exists, I find no evidence to confirm that any of them is now visible. And at only several of the sites is it probable that a light of some kind actually did appear in the distant past. There are, nonetheless, some absolutely fascinating legends—including some major twists from previously encountered tales—associated with the region's ghost lights. For example, despite there being five railroad-related lights, the legend associated with only one of them suggests that a strange light is from the lantern carried by the ghost of a headless revenant. This chapter, perhaps more than any other, spotlights the importance of folklore (and occasional *fake*lore) and the varied contributions of vivid imaginations in the evolution of spooky ghost light tales.

Table 5. Central NC Ghost Lights

Community	County	Light	Environment
Badin	Stanly	Old Whitney Train Track	Railroad
Concord	Cabarrus	Campbell's Ghost	Railroad
Craven	Rowan	File's Store	Cemetery
Durham	Durham	Catsburg Store	Railroad (tracks removed)
Eden/ Wentworth	Rockingham	Eden/Berry Hill	Railroad
Union Grove	Yadkin	Forbush Road	Terrain
Wendell	Wake	Morphus Bridge	Bridge
Yadkinville	Yadkin	Phantom Headlights	Roadway

Badin (Stanly County):
Old Whitney Train Track Light (railroad)

Approximately 5 miles northwest of Badin or 2.5 miles east of New London, Old Whitney Road branches off NC Highway 740 in a northeasterly direction. In about 2.5 miles, the road

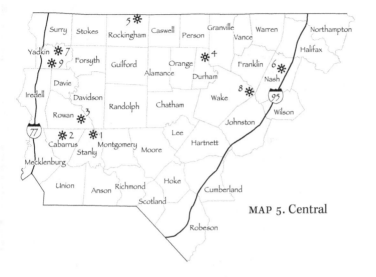

MAP 5. Central

dead ends at the boat ramp on Baden Lake. Lights reportedly appeared on or near an unspecified railroad trestle.

Trying to track down the Old Whitney Train Track Light reminds me of *matryoshka,* the Russian nesting dolls. In the case of this light, the deeper I dug for information, the smaller the leads got, until eventually little if anything was left. Where to begin? Most information on the lights reportedly seen from a railroad trestle seems to be from a single source—the website of Southern Spooks, a paranormal research group. Unfortunately, as so often is the case, the article is undated, and there is no indication of their source of information. The item, however, was updated in 2009. This suggests that it preceded K. M. Simpson's October 2010 article, "Hauntings at the Old Whitney Train Tracks & Trestle." Wording of the Simpson piece is nearly identical to that published earlier by the Southern Spooks research team.

Unfortunately, the Simpson item provides no new information. Compounding the mystery is the fact that there is no mention of a ghost light at Old Whitney Road in the comprehensive *Ghosts of America* website, or, for that matter, in any other source of which I am aware.

The primary reference to a light, which appears verbatim in both of the aforementioned articles, states: "Brave fishermen going catfish[ing] late at night have witnessed unexplainable lights lingering down the tracks." Even stranger, there is mention of what appeared to be "a man . . . forming from a ball of bright light that had a reflection."

So, based on the only known reports, we are led to believe that strange lights appear "down the tracks," and a human image forms from a ball of bright light, also in association with the tracks. But this information begs the questions: Which set of tracks? At what distance? Looking in what direction(s)? What was the physical appearance of the light(s)?

A site visit disclosed that there are two sets of railroad tracks in the immediate vicinity of the boat ramp located at the end of Old Whitney Road. From there, they run in a generally southeasterly direction, and one continues to the northwest. Both however, follow the lake, have trestles, and certainly are used by fishermen. The only possible clue to location is reference to a trestle on the set of tracks leading to the Alcoa plant in Badin. If correct, the light—if seen at all—would appear to someone on the easternmost tracks (those farthest out in the lake).

In an attempt to tie together some of the many loose ends, I wrote to several law enforcement agencies. Surprisingly, perhaps, neither of those who responded had ever heard of ghost lights seen from the Old Whitney tracks or, for that matter, anywhere else in their area of jurisdiction. Another informant talked with two lifelong residents of the area, and they, too, had never heard of the light. Most helpful, however, was Jonathan Underwood, director of the Stanly County Museum in Albemarle. Underwood actually knew someone who claimed to have seen the light—Fred Morgan, who, unfortunately, is deceased. Morgan wrote a series of books on folklore of the Uwharries, the low and very ancient mountains that extend across portions of Stanly and several adjacent counties. Underwood may have solved the mystery, noting, "I've checked on this several times, and several of us are beginning to think that this [light] may have been 'invented' for use in a series of publications on folk legends from the Uwharries." Ironically, no legend seems to have arisen in association with the Old Whitney Train Track Light. Yet it appears that the light itself was deliberately created as an entry in a book on Uwharrie folk legends.

And the Uwharries? They are said to be the oldest mountains in the United States, having withstood the forces of erosion for more than five hundred million years. This fascinating bit of geological history, alone, warrants a visit to Stanly County.

Concord (Cabarrus County). Campbell's Light [Concord Ghost Light] (railroad)

Concord is located at the junction of US 29 and 601 with NC 73 just south of I-85. The old Concord railroad depot, where the light supposedly appeared, no longer exists.

According to two newspaper accounts, both dated December 14, 1888, a fatal accident occurred near the Concord railroad depot on December 4, ten days before the articles appeared. While climbing a ladder between two rail cars, brakeman Alexander Campbell slipped and fell from the train, was run over, and died soon thereafter. Here, however, the tale takes an interesting twist (at least for North Carolina railroad-related ghost lights)—there is no mention of his head being severed. According to the *Concord Times* article, soon after the accident happened, a ghostly light began to appear at the Concord depot. It also notes that when a train reached the spot where the brakeman fell and was killed, "the engineer saw a lantern waving in front of him. He stopped the train when the light went out. He then passed on and looking back saw the light again waving. The train hands refused to go back to examine, and they of course believed it was the ghost of the dead brakeman."

According to Tony Reevy (in his book *Ghost Train!*), the light was widely known and "said to appear nightly at the switch where Campbell was killed and give the same danger signal." In this context, it is interesting to note that nowhere have I found reference to Campbell giving a signal at the time of the accident (remember, he slipped from a ladder between two cars). This part of the legend appears to have evolved without factual basis.

If it existed at all, Campbell's Light seems to have vanished by the end of the nineteenth century, as have memories of its ghostly appearance. In this context, Reevy posed an insightful, yet unanswered, question: "Why did [this] ghost light fade away while others seem to have survived to the present day?" To which I would add: Why did the legend fade away as well? Legends usually linger on long after the ghost lights on which they are based have vanished.

Craven (Rowan County):
No known name [File's Store] (cemetery)

The small settlement of Craven is located on Bringle Ferry Road, approximately seven miles east-southeast of Salisbury. The specific location of the once-reported light is unknown.

Under the best of conditions, a cemetery can be a foreboding place in which any number of strange and scary happenings can occur—particularly to those who believe in ghosts and are easily spooked. If a burial ground has a sinister history, it is even more apt to spawn a legend relating to some hair-raising supernatural condition or event. The Craven area ghost light is one of a handful within the state that is associated with a cemetery. And it is the only such site at which a light reportedly appeared on a regular basis and, in this case, perhaps for more than a century. Despite its association with a graveyard and remarkable longevity, I find no legend associated with the illumination. The lights simply were said to be the shimmering of restless ghosts.

Most information on the Craven light appeared in a 1965 (Raleigh) *News & Observer* article by Heath Thomas. According to his account, "Sometime more than a hundred years ago, [or before 1865] a local resident, John Eller, brutally murdered two women, whom he buried in shallow, unmarked graves. Not long thereafter, a light, big and brighter than a full moon[,] began to appear." As described, the light rose above the graves and surrounding tree tops before sinking back to earth and vanishing. In a slightly different description, the strange illumination is said to rise "flaming like a brushpile [*sic*] on fire," roll along the ground for about a quarter mile, and enter the basement of the then torn-down (or burned-down, according to one version) house once occupied by Eller. According to this account, until at least 1965 when the Thomas article appeared, the lights appeared regularly and as frequently as ten times a night.

A second and quite different tale appears in a 1993 article in the *Salisbury Post* written by Timothy Ball. His rendition of the legend places the light in the vicinity of an old slave cemetery, and there is no mention of John Eller or of the murdered women. Ball's description, which possibly was inspired by the earlier Thomas account, also suggests a long and reliable history of the light's appearance. He describes a large and very bright light of unknown origin. Evidently, the light—like so many others—vanished sometime after the mid-1960s. The several people in the area with whom I spoke were either unaware of the light or had heard vague tales about it from their parents or grandparents. Writing in 1993, Ball noted that, "Recent residents haven't heard of the light, or, if they have, they mention distant car lights."

If, indeed, the light did appear regularly and as many as ten times in a single night, it is difficult to suggest a source. I am unaware of a similar light description anyplace else in the United States. The reported size and frequency of appearance, in particular, make the light extremely unique. The single suggested source, automobile lights, can be easily discounted. There were no cars to travel Bringle Ferry Road in the 1860s. But even more mystifying is the fact that the graveyard from which the light reportedly appeared to rise is located only about 250 yards from Bringle Ferry Road. Yet according to Ball, "no one has [ever] walked back there to find out the truth." So much for curiosity! Oh, and one other thing: the Ball article appeared on October 30, twenty-eight years after the first and only other known reference to the light. Might this suggest that reference to the light was nothing more than an imaginative Halloween hoax? Stranger things certainly have happened.

Durham (Durham County):
Catsburg Store (railroad—tracks removed)

The long abandoned Catsburg Store is located north of Durham at the junction of Old Oxford and Hamlin Roads about 1.5 miles northeast of Braggtown, which is on US 501B.

The Catsburg Country Store, built in the 1920s by Durham County Sheriff Eugene "Cat" Blevins, remains a well-known local landmark with an intriguing legend, or, more correctly, legends. According to one account, a man crossing the railroad tracks near the store was struck by a train and decapitated. But here the story takes a strange twist from the usual scenario; his ghost appears as a headless horseman who, it is said, comes thundering up the tracks at full gallop precisely on the stroke of midnight. (Perhaps the ghost of the headless horseman of Sleepy Hollow rides again, this time in North Carolina where he came to experience a bit of southern hospitality?) In another version, related by Tony Reevy, a high school student and his grandmother were killed at the railroad crossing on Hamlin Road very near the store. Strangely, there seems to be no associated legend tying this second version to the appearance of a light. A third variant lacks mention of a grizzly death but tells of an eerie ghost train that appeared occasionally before the tracks went out of service in 1983 and were removed soon thereafter.

As reported by both Reevy and Ann Green, some local residents claimed that if one stood on the tracks where they cross Hamlin Road and looked down the rails in an easterly direction (or later down the railroad right-of-way) toward Old Oxford Road, a strange light appeared. It resembled a

Catsburg Store

car headlight, only larger, and seemed to be less than a mile away. Based on this description, the probable source of the light is easily explained. Lights of vehicles traveling toward Durham on Old Oxford Road at a distance of about one mile certainly would have been briefly visible until the mid-1980s when vegetation growing in the abandoned right-of-way began to block the view.

Reevy may have solved the mystery. Citing Phil Petty, who was a regular visitor to the Catsburg Store, neither the informant nor the store owners actually believed in any version of the various tales. Rather, they considered them to be nothing more than "amusing local legend[s]." They admitted, no doubt reluctantly, to never having seen a headless horseman, a ghost train, an unexplained distant light, or any other spooky phenomenon in the vicinity. As for the lights seen by viewers looking eastward down the tracks, certainly the local residents recognized them as being headlights of passing vehicles.

Eden-Wentworth (Rockingham County):
Eden or Berry Hill Light (railroad)

Based on available information it is difficult, if not impossible, to determine where this light supposedly appears. Eden and Wentworth are small North Carolina communities in Rockingham County northwest of Reidsville. Berry Hill is located about one-half mile into Virginia, just north of Berry Hill Road (NC 770; county highway 863 in VA). A railroad does cross the highway on the Virginia side about one mile from the state line.

All known references to the Berry Hill Light refer to Eden and Wentworth. Further investigation, however, suggests that the light may be in Virginia—if, indeed, it exists (or existed) at all. I have found only three very brief references to a strange light, and as so often happens, the wording in each of them is identical, suggesting a single initial source from which others copied. After mentioning the occasional sighting of ghosts in a small plantation cemetery near Blue [*sic*] Berry Hill (whoever added the "Blue" must have been unduly influenced by the classic Fats Domino song of the 1960s—the site is Berry Hill), each account states, "The railroad track down the road [from the plantation cemetery] is also haunted. People who drive across these late at night see strange lights and apparitions." That's it; no additional details are mentioned. There is no reference to a source of information, which makes the tale rather suspect. Furthermore, no mention is made of a specific location, the date of earliest (or any other) sighting, or of the light's physical appearance. And of perhaps greatest significance, no extraordinary legend appears to have evolved in association with the light. Where is a lantern-toting, head-searching ghost when needed?

No one with whom I communicated was aware of any strange light sightings during recent decades, although several people recalled having heard of sightings in the distant past. There is a Berry Hill and a nearby plantation located quite near the point where the railroad crosses the highway. No obvious light source is evident, however, in either a northerly or southerly direction along the railroad right-of-way.

So we are left with yet another elusive ghost light and lingering unsolved mystery. Should you be traveling Berry Hill Road on a dark night, I urge you to pause for a moment where the road crosses the tracks and look in both directions. Who knows, you might see a strange light flickering in the distance. Or, if no light appears, according to local lore you might get a glimpse of the ghosts of long-departed slaves said to haunt the small cemetery near the tracks, or possibly a ghostly lady dressed in white believed by some to appear in the nearby plantation house. But don't linger! A local resident has a well-earned reputation for not taking kindly to gawkers or trespassers.

Union Grove (Yadkin County):
Forbush Road (terrain)

Union Grove is a small community located about five miles north-northeast of Yadkinville. Forbush Road intersects Nebo Road one-half mile northeast of town.

The only reference I have found to a ghost light on Forbush Road appears in Frances Casstevens's book, *Ghosts of the North Carolina Piedmont.* As she tells the story, a Mr. Ad-

Union Grove/Forbush Road

ams once lived on the "right side" (going in which direction?) of Forbush Road and about two hundred yards from a dangerous curve (of which there are several). Adams claimed to see a strange glowing light that moved about three feet above the ground from a wooded area, across his front yard, and back into the woods. He claimed that it never deviated from this track. Evidently, the light was rather shy; it vanished if anyone approached it or shined a light in its direction.

The light's source was never explained, and it remains a mystery. At one time, some local residents believed that perhaps it was a light warning drivers of dangers lying ahead on the narrow, winding road. Others thought that perhaps someone had died in a wreck and the light was the ghost of the deceased person haunting Adams and/or passersby. It seems rather strange that the light reportedly was actually seen by only a single individual. Unfortunately, I find no other reference to an unexplained illumination anywhere in the area. And the light—like so many others—seems to have faded, as have memories of its possible shining at some undisclosed time and unknown location in the distant past.

Wendell (Wake County):
Morphus Bridge Light (bridge)

Wendell is located at the intersection of US 64 and NC 231 about fifteen miles east of Raleigh. Morphus Bridge Road branches eastward off US 64 at the east edge of town. The bridge crosses Little River two miles east of Wendell.

The most informative account of the Morphus Bridge Light appears in Roger Manley's fascinating book, *Weird Carolinas*. He devotes one brief paragraph to the light, and, unfortunately, does not indicate his source of information. Evidently, as so often is the case with ghost lights, there are several versions of what supposedly happened at Morphus Bridge during the mid-1940s. Several websites, for example, that predate the 2007 publication of Manley's book basically tell the same heartrending story, which in some ways at least is similar to that of the "Screaming Bridge" near Williamston (chapter 3).

At some unspecified date during the 1940s, a family of three was on its way home from church services. Traveling in a powerful rainstorm, the vehicle went into a skid as it reached Morphus Bridge. The father, who was driving, was unable to control the slide, and the car plunged off the bridge into the deep waters of Little River. It is unclear which of the family members died. Regardless, as the legend goes, late at night one can hear their agonized screams. In one very important way, however, the Manley account differs from others. It adds "and sometimes [nighttime travelers crossing the bridge] even see the headlights of their sunken car still glowing down in the murky water."

A number of the comments that appear in the Morphus Bridge entry on the *Real Haunts* website were posted by local residents. None of them claims to have heard the screams and cries or to have seen lights shining from the riverbed or elsewhere in the vicinity of the bridge. So we seem to have yet another eerie legend of unknown origin, which morphed into various versions and, no doubt, originated as an imaginative light in someone's mind rather than as an actual luminous feature occasionally beaming from the depths of Little River.

Yadkinville (Yadkin County):
Phantom Headlights (roadway)

Location is not specified, other than occurring in Yadkinville at the end of a dead-end road named after an assassinated US president.

I am always extremely skeptical of ghost lights for which information appears in only a single source. This is particularly true when the light's location is left pretty much to the imagination, no dates are given, no family names are mentioned, and no record exists of a fatal accident that supposedly occurred. Furthermore, if a ghost light or accompanying ghostly legend is ingrained in an area's local lore, information about the phenomenon usually can be found on a number of websites.

To my knowledge, the tale of the "Phantom Headlights" appears only in Michael Renegar's book, *Roadside Revenants: And Other North Carolina Ghosts and Legends.* He tells of an accident that happened at the end of a "dead end road—one of several area roads named for an assassinated United States President." Supposedly, police were in hot pursuit of a

Phantom Headlights Yadkinville

fugitive from the law, who led them on a high-speed chase up the narrow road. Little did the miscreant know that a dead end (figuratively and literally) loomed a short distance away at the top of the hill. Unable to stop, his car crashed through the barricade and plunged down the steep slope into the valley below. The police, gazing down on the fatal wreck, saw a huge tree-formed cross that towered grotesquely above the smoldering wreckage. Today, according to the legend, those who view the accident site at night will be followed closely by threatening headlights as they leave. Strangely, the lights are said to appear without a driver or even an accompanying car.

Fascinated by the tale, I visited Yadkinville on a crisp February day in 2012. Putting together pieces of the story, I believed that McKinley Road was the most logical site (President McKinley was assassinated in 1901). It branches off

Hoots Road, which was mentioned in Renegar's account. And sure enough, the narrow and winding McKinley Road ends abruptly just a short distance from and high above US Highway 421 in the valley below. So far, so good, right?

After visiting the site, I visited briefly with several residents whose homes are located at or near the end of McKinley. They had never heard of an accident on the street and were unaware of any ghost light that supposedly haunted their neighborhood. Inquiries directed at the County Historical Society, a local librarian, and personnel at the Yadkinville Chamber of Commerce also drew blanks.

Generally speaking, law enforcement personnel are reluctant to respond to questions pertaining to ghost lights. I'm sure they do not want to provide any information that might encourage people to snoop around either residential or remote and potentially dangerous areas at night. In this instance, however, I am extremely grateful to the Yadkinville Police Department for the detailed information provided by one of its officers. Basically, he was unaware of any such legend in the area or of any fatal accident on McKinley Road (or any other street in the city named for an assassinated president).

Here, however, the information provided by the officer takes an interesting turn. A short distance south of McKinley Road and across Hoots Road is Neelie Road. At a point near Deep South Creek, the road makes a sharp turn. Local legend holds that a ghost car mysteriously chases unsuspecting drivers and tries to run them off the road. A short distance south of the creek, Rudy Road branches in a westerly direction off Neelie. For decades, those traveling Rudy Road on a clear night could see an astonishing sight. Looming above the roadway was an old tree, the trunk and lower branches of which formed an almost perfect cross. It appears that the Phantom Headlights legend grew from the combination of a local tale, a naturally formed cross, and Michael Renegar's wonderfully creative ability to spin a fascinating and spine-tingling yarn.

Chapter Six

WESTERN

⚡ ⚡ ⚡

ESTERN NORTH CAROLINA is a region of superlatives. As one travels westward across the state, the
Carolina Piedmont gradually gives way to higher
and higher Appalachian ridges and peaks. They include Mt.
Mitchell, which, at an elevation of 6,684 feet, is the highest
point in North America east of South Dakota's Black Hills. It
is a region of spectacular natural beauty, where picturesque
villages lie nestled in valleys wedged between uplands, the
slopes of which are softly rounded by several hundred million years of erosion. Higher elevations offer sprawling vistas that stretch to distant horizons, a view interrupted occasionally only by the haze responsible for the mountains'
nickname, the "Smokies." As one would expect, judging from
the terrain, population density diminishes the farther west
one goes. In some locations, it is possible to see distances of
twenty, thirty, or more miles. Such views often span a densely
forested landscape that sprawls over an area of several hundred square miles without revealing a single tell-tale sign of
human presence or activity.

Primarily because of the rolling topography and the sweeping vistas that it affords, at least eight of the fourteen ghost

lights reported in the West are terrain related. They include the famous Brown Mountain Lights, which by any measure rank among the nation's (if not the world's) most spectacular light displays. And a mysterious light I saw from the Thomas Divide Overlook on the Blue Ridge Parkway north of Cherokee was sensational and absolutely defied explanation. The West also includes some of the state's most intriguing ghost light legends. So enjoy your travels through the fascinating and picturesque landscapes of western North Carolina. Your trip will include beautiful scenery, picturesque villages, and, hopefully, some unforgettable ghost light displays.

TABLE 6. Western NC Ghost Lights

Community	County	Light	Environment
Big Laurel	Unknown	Unidentified	Unknown
Blowing Rock	Watauga	Historical	Terrain
Cedar Mountain	Transylvania	Green River Preserve	Terrain
Cherokee	Swain	Thomas Divide Overlook	Terrain
Chimney Rock Pass	Rutherford	Historical Sighting	Terrain
Cullowhee	Jackson	Wayehutta (1)	Terrain
Cullowhee	Jackson	Wayehutta (2)	Terrain
Hewitt	Swain	Mud Cut	Railroad
Hot Springs	Madison	Shut-In-Creek	Terrain
Morganton	Burke	Brown Mountain	Terrain
Plumtree	Avery	Slippery Hill	Cemetery
Rutherfordton	Rutherford	Gilboa Church	Cemetery
Statesville	Iredell	Bostian's Bridge	Railroad
Statesville	Iredell	No name	Railroad

MAP 6. Western

Big Laurel (unknown county):
No known name (unknown)

Other than "Big Laurel," it is impossible to determine a location based on the information available.

A several-year attempt to track down the ghost lights reportedly seen near Big Laurel proved to be incredibly frustrating and as elusive as, well, chasing ghosts. In *Atlas of the Mysterious in North America,* Rosemary Ellen Guiley lists a total of only forty-four ghost light locations in the entire United States and Canada. Strangely, her list includes a very brief mention of lights supposedly seen in Big Laurel, North Carolina. Of the illuminations, she simply states, "Two to three moving lights near here." That's it! She provided no additional information. In what I consider to be the most detailed and informative book on ghost light phenomena, *Illuminating the Darkness: The Mystery of Spook Lights,* Dale Kaczmarek also lists Big Laurel as one of the fourteen ghost lights in the state. About the lights, he only states, "There have been reports of two to three moving lights seen near here." So we are left with one brief sentence, stated almost verbatim, in perhaps the two most comprehensive and reliable sources of Northern America's ghost light information. I have never found any other reference—except for several websites that quote Guiley and/or Kaczmarek verbatim—to a strange light in or near Big Laurel, North Carolina. Further compounding the problem, Guiley did not provide a source for the scant data she presented, and Kaczmarek simply copied (and cited) Guiley. And oddly, no legend is associated with the light, which casts further doubt on its existence.

In the case of Big Laurel, many critical questions obviously remain unanswered. For example, where is Big Laurel? The US Board of Geographic Names lists ten features in North Carolina with that name. Near which Big Laurel do the lights supposedly appear? Is it a mountain peak in Clay County, a creek in Madison County, a waterfall in Macon County, or some other physical feature? Or is it the Big Laurel settlement in Madison County or the one in Swain County? Where did the lights appear relative to Big Laurel; that is, what was their exact location? When were the lights seen and by whom? What was their appearance? Were two or three lights seen repeatedly, or did they appear only a single time? And, of greatest importance, where did Guiley get her information, and why did she not cite its source?

I was able to communicate with several long-time residents of both Big Laurel settlements. They had never heard of a ghost light in or near their community. I also was unable to find information suggesting the presence of a ghost light near any of the natural features named Big Laurel. Here, however, the search takes an interesting geographical twist. "Big Laurel" is a common place-name throughout the Appalachian region, where the beautiful flowering shrub is known by its perhaps more familiar name, rhododendron.

In his book *Tales of Kentucky Ghosts,* William Montell tells of strange lights that once appeared regularly near Big Laurel (Harlan County), Kentucky. Could North Carolina's Big Laurel lights be the result of shoddy research and a mistaken geographical location? Stranger things have happened.

Blowing Rock (Watauga County):
No known name (terrain)

Blowing Rock is on US Highways 221 and 321, approximately seven miles south of Boone. Specific sites mentioned below are Linville Ridge, located near Grandfather Mountain off NC Highway 105 some twelve miles west of Blowing Rock, and the Saddle Hills development on US 221 about two miles west of Blowing Rock.

The view from any high vantage point in this part of North Carolina is spectacular. Looking southward from Linville Ridge or the Saddle Hills development, a broad panoramic view unfolds off the Blue Ridge Mountains and adjacent valleys. The horizon vanishes gradually as it disappears in the smoky haze that gave these peaks their nickname. Given the region's rugged terrain and the vast vistas it affords, it is little wonder that several area residents claim to have seen strange lights flashing above the distant mountains.

As is true of nearly all ghost lights, accounts of those reportedly seen from two vantage points in this area raise more questions than they provide answers. For example, despite months of searching, I found but a single key reference to the lights—and it is the source from which all other accounts were taken. On August 31, 1988, an article by Mike Hannah appeared in the (Boone) *Watauga Democrat.* Hannah reported that on August 23, 1987, three (unnamed) couples at Linville Ridge saw strange lights in the distance, the flashes of which lit the sky behind Grandfather Mountain. As described, the lights "sometimes resembled lightning ... [but] looked more like fireworks than any natural lightning they had ever seen."

A year later, a doctor and his wife living in the Saddle Hills development also claimed to have seen strange lights in the distance. As explained to Hannah, they appeared for a second or two as "orange-pinkish" flashes of light that "rose up and shimmered almost like fireworks." In this context, as will be disclosed later, I believe that it is quite significant that they discounted the possibility of lightning simply because no sound accompanied the display. The couple claimed that no one else saw the lights, a factor they found quite surprising.

As I said, all information was taken from a single source, the 1988 article in the *Watauga Democrat*. But surprisingly, I first learned of the lights seen from near Blowing Rock from two other sources. Once again, Rosemary Ellen Guiley, in *Atlas of the Mysterious in North America*, included Blowing Rock as one of only six ghost lights in all of North Carolina. And again, she did not cite her source of information, although it was taken pretty much word-for-word from the Hannah article. Additionally, Kaczmarek included the lights as one of the fourteen he listed for the state, and his description is nearly verbatim to Guiley's, which he cites as his source of information.

So, what are we left with? There is but a single newspaper account, relating sightings by a total of eight people, who within the span of a single year witnessed very brief flashes of light that they were unable to explain. Yet based on this meager information, the lights seen from near Blowing Rock are now deeply etched into both Northern America's and North

Carolina's ghost light lore. Interestingly enough, no legend evolved to explain the sightings. Perhaps contemporary society is too well-educated and sophisticated to formulate bizarre tales?

Initially, there was some speculation that the flashes might have been the Brown Mountain Lights. As described, however, the lights were "well up in the sky," unlike most accounts of the display seen at the famous ghost light location about fifteen miles to the south. On numerous occasions, I have seen lights similar to those described and am quite sure that it was distant lightning strikes that the witnesses saw and were unable to identify. The vista from the purported viewing sites is spectacular, spanning a distance of perhaps fifty miles. On a dark and stormy night, clouds from which the lightning flashed would not be visible, and at a considerable distance claps of thunder would not be audible. A spectacular light display, yes. But unexplained ghost lights? Extremely doubtful.

Cedar Mountain (Transylvania County):
Green River Preserve [No known name] (terrain)

Green River Preserve is a youth camp near Cedar Mountain, off US 276 southeast of Brevard. At Cedar Mountain, go east on Cascade Lake Road for about fifty yards and turn right on Reasonover Road. The pavement ends in four miles; turn right on Green River Road for about a third of a mile to the camp.

Imagine attending a camp counselors' meeting on a pleasant summer evening when suddenly a big, bright, smooth ball of light moves along a trail, passes by your startled group, continues along for a short distance, and simply vanishes into thin air. As described by camp owner, Sandy Schenck, this is precisely what happened in the summer of 1991. The light was so bright that the group was sure it was carried by someone coming up the trail. This theory, however, was soon abandoned when the light's brightness clearly revealed that it was not carried by a human.

Folk wisdom suggests that lightning never strikes twice in the same place (don't you believe it!). Of course, there is no way of knowing whether ball lightning was involved in this sighting. Nonetheless, according to Schenck, the following summer another counselors' meeting was interrupted by a large ball of light that suddenly appeared at a distance of about fifty yards from the campsite. As the counselors watched the mysterious orb, it split into two lights, one seemingly stacked above the other. Then another light suddenly appeared, stacked above the two others. The three lights were so bright that they cast a shadow. Then they, too, mysteriously vanished as rapidly as they had appeared.

According to many old-timers, before electricity was introduced to the area, Jack-o'-Lanterns appeared quite frequently. You may recall from chapter 1 that these lights (also called Will-o'-the-Wisp, or *ignus fatuus*) are believed to be caused by marsh gasses, methane and phosphine. Seen throughout much of the world, the resulting lights most frequently are described as resembling flickering flames. This description, however, does not coincide with that of the strange lights seen by the counselors at the Green River Preserve Camp. After the two sightings more than a quarter century ago, the lights were never seen again. Based on the descriptions, it is possible that they were ball lightning, but we will never know for sure what caused them.

If you happen to be in the surrounding Dupont State Forest during late spring, you may be treated to a somewhat different spectacular light display—the mating glow of thousands of Blue Ghost fireflies. Their pale blue glow seems to float just above the ground, creating a lighted carpet on the forest floor that, according to one description, resembles Christmas lights. Now that is a ghostly light worth seeing!

Cherokee (Swain County):
Thomas Divide Overlook (terrain)

Thomas Divide Overlook (TDO) is north of Cherokee on the Blue Ridge Parkway (Milepost 464), 5.1 miles east of the junction with US 441. The community and overlook are located on the Qualla Reservation of the Eastern Band of Cherokee. The overlook is named for the only white chief of the Cherokee and the individual responsible for the establishment of the Qualla Reservation, William Holland Thomas. It is most unfortunate that the view from TDO is severely restricted by foliage during much of the year. The best view is during the winter dormant season.

The view from TDO is absolutely spectacular. Spread out both high above and far below the viewer is a vast panorama of mountains and valleys covering an area of a hundred or more square miles. Most amazing is that, with one very minor exception (what appear to be two structures in the distance), there is absolutely no visible evidence of human presence when viewed during the day. It is at night that the view from the overlook can come to life and offer some very strange sights.

On my first visit to TDO, I was treated to a fascinating display of lights that seemed to appear in three widely separated locations and with vastly different appearances. In one location far to the west, a number of white lights appeared in rather rapid succession and within a very small area as dusk

Thomas Divide Overlook on Blue Ridge Parkway

Thomas Divide Overlook (winter) on Blue Ridge Parkway

settled upon the distant mountain crest. Mysteriously, the white lights suddenly vanished, some only to be replaced immediately by somewhat dimmer lights of blood-red color. Most of the white lights were visible for less than one minute before they vanished. The red lights disappeared in a matter of seconds. This seemed incredibly strange, to say the least.

A second set of lights appeared periodically to the immediate left (west) of the overlook. They flashed brightly for a few seconds as they appeared to dart among the trees before mysteriously disappearing. These lights seemed to be quite close, and I'm sure that to at least some viewers they must appear to be quite threatening as viewed from this rather lonely spot.

As a blanket of total darkness began to descend, a third light appeared in the deep valley located northwest of the overlook and at a distance of perhaps two miles. It was quite bright, moved slowly and at a steady velocity, and traveled from north-to-south in a very straight line. Suddenly, the light stopped, but strangely remained fully illuminated for the roughly one hour I remained at the viewing site. At the time, I was quite confident that the light was from a vehicle, perhaps a poacher, or someone who simply stopped to talk with a neighbor in some previously unseen settled area.

While at the site, I took a number of compass readings to record the light's locations as precisely as possible on a detailed map of the area and also made note of the frequency and duration of light sightings. Armed with this information, I was determined to return to Thomas Divide Overlook the next day with answers to the strange sightings. That night, I did my homework, using detailed area maps and Google Earth satellite images in an attempt to explain the lights' source or sources.

I found that there is a road that leads from US 441 to the Clingmans Dome parking lot. And it is located just beneath the crest of the distant mountains—precisely where many other viewers claim to have seen the same light display that I witnessed. It became obvious that the first group of more than a dozen separate lights were from vehicles leaving the parking lot at dusk. As they descended down the sloping lot, their lights shone directly toward TDO. At the base of the lot is a sharp turn, for which many—but not all—drivers brake. Due to a sharp turn at the point vehicles exit the parking lot, headlights vanish abruptly. At a distance of some fifteen miles, tail lights were very dim if visible at all. When drivers apply the brakes as they round the curve, however, the bright red brake lights can be seen. A subsequent visit to the Clingmans Dome parking lot verified my hunch.

The second set of lights, those seen close by and through the trees for several seconds, proved to be from vehicles traveling eastward on the Blue Ridge Parkway. As they round the bend near Raven Fork Overlook at a distance of about one mile, their lights very briefly shine directly toward TDO. This theory was easily confirmed by timing the appearance of lights and the arrival of vehicles at the viewing point less than two minutes later.

I was quite confident that the source of the third light—the one seen in the rugged valley below TDO—also would be easy to identify. But little did I know that I was in for a shocking surprise! Using compass readings and the vertical angle at which the light appeared, I searched in vain for any sign of a road or trail where it was seen. There was none. And not a single sign of human presence could be found on maps or satellite images. Local residents assured me that the area was nothing but remote wilderness, through which no road or trail passed. Additionally, the area is rugged and heavily forested. Had any vehicle moved on the ground, it would have weaved between trees and across rugged terrain. What I saw moved in a very straight line. Furthermore, at no time was the light obstructed, as would be the case if it was from a vehicle moving on the ground through the dense woodland.

There are many reports of "unexplained lights" seen from Thomas Divide Overlook that move about. They include a substantial number of descriptions that vary greatly from the lights I saw. Various viewers have insisted that lights appear in areas where I saw only darkness. In fact, videos exist (see bibliography) of lights that appear in places where they cannot be explained by human presence. Many accounts indicate that lights change in intensity and color, sway back and forth like a lantern, or shoot up like a Roman candle and then fall to the ground. One thing shared by all viewers is the recognition that they witnessed something incredibly spectacular and deeply mysterious. Clearly, lights of unexplained origin do appear here, and, evidently, they are seen on a fairly regular basis judging from the numerous eyewitness accounts.

Mysterious lights seen on distant mountain slopes and surrounding valleys have appeared in the area for a very long time—perhaps centuries. And as you would expect, many legends have evolved through the years to explain them. Cherokee folk-tradition, as is true of nearly all traditional cultures, includes beliefs in witches, ghosts, and other supernatural figures. According to a 1936 article by John Parris, witches take the form of ghost lights that are frequently seen in mountainous areas of the state. One interesting tale tells of the legendary giant, Judaculla, hurling fireballs. At the other extreme of human stature, a folk-belief holds that lights are from lanterns carried by "Little People" believed by some to inhabit the mountain wilderness. A more gruesome legend tells of a Cherokee shaman who rebelled against federal soldiers. He was caught, killed, and his body dismembered with the various parts then spread throughout the area as a warning to others not to defy the US military. The lights, it is said, are his spirit searching for his parts in an attempt to reassemble the body. Some non–Native Americans believe that the lights might be lanterns carried by the ghosts of Civil War soldiers killed in action.

According to Cherokee elders, family tales going back generations suggest that mysterious lights were seen in the area as early as the 1700s, if not before. According to a local paranormal author and investigator, Michael Rivers (as quoted by Hester), the elders believed the lights "are guardians of the mountains and the life secrets of the Cherokee people." To me, this is a far more satisfying hypothesis than one attributing the area's mysterious lights to UFOs, Will-o'-the-Wisps, piezoelectric effects, or spirits wandering about in search of body parts. Regardless of the source, the display seen from Thomas Divide Overlook offers one of the nation's most spectacular, least known—and for some of them, at least—largely unexplained ghost light spectacles.

Chimney Rock Pass (Rutherford County):
Ghost armies (terrain)

Chimney Rock Pass is on US Highway 74, approximately twenty-five miles southeast of Asheville.

Chimney Rock is a well-known rock formation in the Blue Ridge Mountains and home to a popular state park. More than two centuries ago, it was also the site of what certainly must rank as one of the state's strangest apparitions. I include this sighting simply because it offers a splendid example of cultural diffusion—the spread of ideas from place-to-place through time—and the fact that we often tend to see or otherwise experience a phenomenon that is in style at the time.

Accounts vary considerably, but it appears that on the evening of July 31, 1806, six area residents saw what they reported to be "a thousand or ten thousand things flying in the air [that resembled a] very numerous crowd of beings resembling the human species." The "glittering white appearances" (i.e., lights) moved about for nearly an hour before they "vanished out of sight, leaving a solemn and pleasing impression on the mind, accompanied with a diminution of bodily strength." George Newton, a local clergyman, published a description of the strange event in the *Raleigh Register and State Gazette*. The reverend was uncertain whether the sighting was "accountable on philosophical principles" or was a "prelude to the descent of the holy city."

Five years later, in September 1811, the sky above Chimney Rock reportedly was again the scene of an amazing spectacle. As reported to writer and scientific observer Silas McDowell, an elderly farm couple witnessed the spirited "Spectre Battle of Chimney Rock Pass" involving "two opposing armies of horse-men, high up in the air all mounted on winged horses." One commander was even heard to cry "Charge!" after which a ferocious battle ensued with sword blades "glittering and flashing in the setting [s]un's rays" and the clash of swords clearly audible. After a period of about ten minutes, the battle was over and "the shouts of the victors and wails of the defeated were plainly heard."

Explanations of these two sightings are as bizarre as the reported events themselves. In 1831, McDowell was told by a grandson of two viewers that his grandparents had "probably seen a mirage-like optical illusion caused by suspended water droplets in the atmosphere magnifying and distorting images of swarms of gnats." Other suggestions include an aurora borealis and hallucinations (perhaps the result of excessive consumption of that good ol' mountain 'shine?).

I believe that it is quite probable that something strange was seen on the two occasions near Chimney Rock during the early years of the nineteenth century. What specifically appeared no doubt will always remain a mystery. A clue, however, may be found in Charles Fort's fascinating book, *New Lands*. He reported numerous sightings of "phantom soldiers" between the mid-1700s and the late 1800s, mainly in the British Isles, the original homeland of many of the state's early settlers. Fort suggested that "our general acceptance is that all reports upon such phenomena are colored in terms of appearances and subjects uppermost in [our] minds." It appears that the time was an era of phantom soldier sightings, an idea deeply rooted in the folklore of the Old Country that ultimately diffused to (and possibly marched through) the mountains of western North Carolina.

Cullowhee (Jackson County):
Wayehutta [1] (terrain)

Wayehutta Creek flows into the Tuckasegee River on the east side of Cullowhee, home of Western Carolina University. Lights reportedly appeared on the mountainsides bordering both Wayehutta Road, which parallels the creek, and Watson Branch Road, which branches to the left approximately 1.3 miles from the main turn-off. Lights also have been reported at various locations on the opposite slopes of adjacent mountains.

Wayehutta Creek

Stranger things appear to have happened up the Wayehutta than the creek's pronunciation, "Worry-hutt." I am indebted to lifetime Jackson County resident, Norma Clayton, for having shared the following information pertaining to mysterious lights that evidently appeared in the area for at least three generations, if not longer. In addition to her own sightings and those of other family members and acquaintances, some details she related were memories of the light shared by one-time resident Lenoir Cabe.

According to Cabe, the earliest record of sightings came from her grandmother, who during a restless night would watch the mountain lights, which she described as resembling a group of people carrying lanterns that swayed back and forth. They began at the Wayehutta Copper Mine and moved slowly down the mountainside, crossed the road and creek, and then went up the opposite mountain slope.

Clayton recalls seeing the lights on many occasions when she and her sisters spent nights with their grandparents, whose home was farther down the valley from the location described by Cabe. Recounting the sightings, she said they would "huddle beside the bedroom window and watch as the lights flickered and shimmered and seemed to float down the side of the mountain opposite [the] house." She describes them as "dim, white lights that moved in a weaving, bobbing fashion—as if someone was holding a lantern and walking down the hill." At first, she and her sisters wondered if someone was fox hunting up on the ridge as they watched the lights move down the mountainside. This possibility was ruled out, however, because the mountain is very steep where the lights were seen, and it would be impossible for a person to walk down the slope as rapidly as the lights moved.

Strangely, no legend appears to have evolved in reference to the lights, although there is one noteworthy exception. The story as told to Clayton by her grandmother is similar to several others in North Carolina. But let her tell the story. Her grandmother and a group of women were walking down Wayehutta Road when:

Suddenly a light appeared and began to move up the road toward them.... The light moved toward one of the women, stopped in front of her, flickered, and went out. Hurrying down the road they stopped at the first house they came to, which just happened to be the woman's house that the light had singled out. There they found a group of men from the mine waiting on her. Her husband had been killed that afternoon when a large rock fell on him. Then

Mamma and the other women realized what the light had meant—it had been a sign of death.

Clayton noted that her grandmother was of Celtic heritage. A belief in lights being associated with death—either foretelling or immediately following a fatality—was widely held in the United Kingdom. It was introduced into North Carolina as is evident from similar tales associated with several other ghost lights in the state.

Although decades have passed since Clayton last saw the lights, she believes that they still can be seen if one knows where to look. During a trip up the Wayehutta with her, she noted that in many places trees now restrict a view of the mountainsides. This, in fact, may be why there are few if any recent reports of sightings. It seems very likely that whatever caused the lights that shimmered on the mountainsides bordering Wayehutta Creek must still be operative. If you are in the area on a clear night, you might want to drive up Wayehutta Creek Road (which dead ends) to see for yourself whether they are still illuminating the mountainsides with their mysterious glow.

Cullowhee (Jackson County):
Wayehutta [2] (terrain)

(See Wayehutta [1].) Other than along the banks of Wayehutta Creek, the location of the light is unknown.

It is rather amazing how often someone reports seeing a ghostly light display, yet further investigation reveals that he or she may have been the only individual who ever reported seeing the spectacle. This seems to be true in the case of lights that supposedly once appeared along the banks of Wehahutta (as incorrectly spelled in the account) Creek.

I have found but a single reference to these Wayehutta Lights. It is an April 5, 2002, account posted by a Jerry Neal on a website that is no longer active. According to Neal, he "personally witnessed . . . two lights. They start off on opposing sides of the creek bank, around 50 yards or so apart, come toward each other, and spin around each other before merging into one brilliant light. Afterwards, the now one light, goes up into the air, and slowly fades out." And rather amazingly, Neal's alleged sighting even came with an accompanying legend. Before the Civil War, he noted, two young lovers of different races were caught together along the creek. The boy was hanged, and the girl committed suicide. The lights, he claimed, are said to be the souls of the estranged lovers searching for each other and finally coming together each night for, we can assume, eternity.

In the hope of learning more about the lights along Wayehutta Creek, I contacted several longtime Cullowhee residents and the district ranger for the surrounding Nantahala National Forest. None of them had ever heard of either the light or accompanying legend. And all agreed that a considerable number of lights—all from common sources—would be visible from the rather heavily populated Wayehutta Road that borders the creek. In the absence of additional information, I can only conclude that Mr. Neal's ghost light and its associated legend most likely are products of his hyperactive imagination and, perhaps, a Western Carolina University creative writing class.

Hewitt (Swain County) or Old Fort (McDowell County): Mud Cut (railroad)

Mudcut Branch is in Swain County near Hewitt, on US 19 and 74, about twenty-two miles southwest of Bryson City. Take

Hewitt/Mud Cut RR and hill

the dirt road to the Nantahala Chalk & Limestone Company, located immediately west of Ferebee Monument Park. Mud Cut (two words), as mentioned by Tony Reevy, is near the small settlement of Graphite, located approximately five miles northwest of Old Fort on Graphite Road.

The Mud Cut Ghost Light is perhaps best described as being yet another mystery wrapped within a mystery. I first learned of the light from Tony Reevy's book, *Ghost Train!* Mud Cut was an engineering and construction nightmare along the route of the old Western North Carolina Railroad (now Norfolk Southern) located about five miles northwest of Old Fort. As the railroad bed was being excavated, mud kept flowing down the steep adjacent mountainside and blocking the intended route. Finally, after countless loads of debris were removed, the railroad was completed and opened to traffic.

In Reevy's version, soon after the railroad was completed through Mud Cut, local residents claimed to see a pair of legs walking along the tracks. They were illuminated by a ghostly lantern (in the absence of a torso and arms, it is unclear how the lantern was carried). The legs supposedly began their nightly trek at 9:00 p.m. sharp. They strolled to the top of the steep grade then suddenly vanished, only to reappear back where their brief journey had begun. The legend goes on to explain the (partial?) revenant as being the ghost of a man identified only as McCathey, who was killed by his brother Bill in a hunting accident. Here, the tale takes a very strange twist, one rather difficult to believe: Bill evidently mistook his brother for a groundhog, so he shot him.

In my attempt to locate the rather elusive Mud Cut and its even more obscure ghost light, I communicated with numerous people in the area. Most of them were unaware of the land feature, and none of them had ever heard of the nocturnal walking legs or swaying lantern. On one occasion, after having visited Graphite (the small rural settlement located closest to Mud Cut) and on my way back to I-40, while passing through Old Fort I visited the town's excellent Railroad Museum. The staff was very aware of Mud Cut, but no one recalled ever having heard the tale of legs and eerie light.

Frustrated in my attempt to learn more about the Mud Cut Light, I did what I should have done at the very outset—checked to find Reevy's source of information. Was I ever in for a surprise! Readers familiar with the wonderful *Foxfire* series of folk-life books edited by Eliot Wigginton know that the various stories were gathered by high school students in Rabun Gap, Georgia. Among the tales appearing in *Foxfire*

2 was an entry by Mrs. Ardilla Grant, who contributed the story upon which Reevy's entry was based. But there was one very significant difference: she placed Mud Cut, the legs, and the ghostly light in Hewitts [*sic*: Hewitt], a small, unincorporated settlement in Swain County. This, of course, begs the question: How and why did Reevy place the legend at a location nearly one hundred miles to the east?

After reading the Grant account, I visited Hewitt and talked with a gentleman at the Nantahala Chalk & Limestone Company office. Neither he, nor anyone else in the area with whom I spoke, had ever heard of the legend or seen the walking legs and swaying light. I thought to ask, however, if there was a Mud Cut in the area. He pointed to the small nearby stream that flows beneath the railroad tracks and access road and said, "Mudcut Branch." Unfortunately, this leaves unanswered a rather significant question: How, during the 1970s, did a woman in Rabun Gap, Georgia, know about Mudcut Branch and the tale of walking legs and a swaying lantern in a small rural western North Carolina settlement? Additionally, no legend appears to explain the legs and light. This suggests to me, at least, that the entire story is a myth, quite probably a yarn spun by an old-timer eager to tell a wild tale to a group of impressionable Rabun Gap high school students.

Hot Springs (Madison County):
Shut-In-Creek (terrain)

Shut-in-Creek is four miles west of Hot Springs on US highways 25 and 70.

In *Haunted Places: The National Directory,* Dennis Hauck tells a fascinating and rather chilling tale of an enigmatic ghost light that "rolls down hills like a barrel" accompanied by haunting, "disembodied voices." According to Hauck's account, some very strange things have happened on the hillsides bordering Shut-in-Creek. They supposedly began more than a century ago when a man is said to have died from poisonous fumes inhaled at a mine in the area. Adding to the mystery of the "Ghost Lights of Shut-in-Hollow," Hauck's information came from Nancy Roberts's book, *Ghosts of the Southern Mountains & Appalachia.* Unfortunately, her story came from an uncle's brother, identified only as Ben, and without further details or other references to sources.

Initially, I was unable to find any additional information on the light. Email messages to several library and local law enforcement personnel went unanswered. However, a librarian at Mars Hill College suggested that I contact a local architect, Taylor Barnhill. Barnhill showed considerable interest in my research and was extremely helpful in providing important information pertaining to several lights, including the rolling barrel of Shut-in-Hollow. Not long after our original exchanges of communication, I received the following note from him:

> Taylor . . . I have to admit that I made up the "Ghosts of Shut-in-Hollow" just to fit the Halloween story, "Legend of Sleepy Hollow." But we do have plenty of screech owls that sound plenty weird. (Signed: John Gebhards)

I can only wonder how many other ghost light tales and their accompanying legends had a similar origin. By definition, folklore is faceless; the origin of nearly all folktales is unknown, with sources almost always being anonymous. Here, however, we have a very simple, yet unusual, example of a supposed ghost light and accompanying story that is traced to its source. Equally surprising is that Shut-in-Hollow is one of only five North Carolina ghost lights mentioned by Hauck in his national directory of haunted places.

Morganton (Burke County):
Brown Mountain Lights (terrain)

This marvelous display of lights is visible from a number of locations. The three most common viewing sites are Brown Mountain Overlook, a clearly marked parking area located on NC 181, 20 miles north of Morganton; Wiseman's View, a rather remote but clearly marked site located about 5 miles south of Linville Falls on the rather narrow, rugged, gravel NC route 1238 (a sign indicates the location of this road at its junction with NC 183, which is 0.7 miles off US 221 on NC 183); and Lost Cove Cliffs Overlook at Milepost 310 on the Blue Ridge Parkway, 2 miles north of the NC Highway 181 intersection.

It was a beautiful autumn evening when I first drove northward out of Morganton on NC 181 hoping to see the famous Brown Mountain Lights (BMLs) put on their spectacular display. Over the years, I had read hundreds of pages of literature devoted to their mysterious appearance, possible sources, and related legends. As you can imagine, it was with excited anticipation that I looked forward to viewing what many observers consider to be the most spectacular ghost light display in the South, if not in the entire country. I know of no other lights in the world about which more has been written, or which have been subjected to greater scientific scrutiny. They are enshrined in the lyrics of a popular song, "Legend of the Brown Mountain Lights," penned by Scotty Wiseman and sung by a number of well-known folk and country artists. They also have received widespread discussion in various media, including at least one national television program devoted to paranormal phenomena.

Brown Mountain viewing spot

Brown Mountain with terrain appearing above south end (this is where hundreds of lights are seen)

Brown Mountain with sign to Wisemans View

Brown Mountain, Wisemans View

Yet, as I approached the viewing site, I must admit to having been somewhat apprehensive, not really knowing what to expect. The literature, videos, and other accounts of the BMLs present a kaleidoscopic array of contradictions. For example, the various sources of information (including videos) literally include an "A-to-Z" range of descriptions. There seems to be no agreement whatsoever in regard to the number, color, size, shape, location, or movement of the lights. This leads one to wonder which of the lights, among the hundreds seen, are the real Brown Mountain Lights? The same holds true in regard to when the lights are most apt to appear, the conditions under which they are seen, and where to look for the real lights relative to the location of the mountain itself. Some sources indicate that the lights appear nightly when visibility allows, whereas others suggest that they rarely appear. Many sources suggest that the lights are seen only above and beyond the mountain; others suggest that the real lights appear only on the dark, western, viewer-facing side of the ridge. Contradictions such as these abound and certainly are confusing.

One thing about the Brown Mountain Lights is abundantly clear: although they have illuminated the nighttime sky for centuries, they remain a baffling mystery. When viewing the lights, what the individual observer sees, believes to be the "real" lights, and both interprets and describes as such, seems to depend much more on individual perceptions rather than on the lights' physical reality.

As I approached the overlook my anticipation grew. One thing seemed certain: on this clear, cool, calm October evening, conditions were perfect for the lights to appear and to present their spectacular display. And as the evening progressed, I certainly was not disappointed! Dusk was falling

Brown Mountain from Lost Cove Cliffs on Blue Ridge Parkway

when I arrived at the overlook. The viewing area already was occupied by a number of vehicles and about two dozen people. Stretched out below at a distance of several miles was Brown Mountain, a long, relatively low, north-south oriented hogback ridge. In this context, it is very important to keep in mind that an awareness of local terrain is extremely important if one is to understand the incredible light display that appears as darkness falls. The Highway 181 Overlook is at an elevation of 2,800 feet. Brown Mountain varies from a high of 2,726 feet at its northern edge to about 2,400 feet at its southern extremity. Because of differences in elevation on and surrounding the mountain, as seen from this overlook nearly all lights appear *above* and *behind* the mountain and only over the lower southern half of the ridge.

As the light began to fade, several people suddenly shouted in excited unison, "There it is!" Looking up, I saw a single white light clinging to the distant hillsides that form a backdrop above and beyond Brown Mountain. Then, in rapid succession, there appeared another, then another, and still another; dozens of lights seemed to be popping up everywhere. Within a relatively short period of time complete darkness fell, and the distant Catawba Valley and background adjacent hillsides were transformed into a wonderland of hundreds, if not thousands, of sparkling lights. Some were stationary, whereas others moved either horizontally or vertically. Most were white or red, but other colors appeared as well. A few lights shone brightly for a few moments, then vanished. It was a magnificent sight and one that certainly provided ample fuel to feed one's imagination.

As mentioned above, the BMLs may have been subjected to more scientific research than any other ghost light in the United States. A century ago, two US Geological Survey–sponsored studies concluded that the lights were from common sources: vehicles, towns, rural settlements, fires, and so forth. Clearly, this explanation holds true for the vast majority of lights that appear above and beyond the mountain. As a scientist and somewhat of a skeptic, I must admit to having held an initial belief that all BMLs could easily be explained as emanating from ordinary sources. Little did I know at the time that Brown Mountain still held deep secrets that would be revealed on this night and during my several subsequent visits. And the things that I saw not only posed a severe challenge to my initial skepticism, they also defied explanation based on any possible source of which I was aware.

On this first trip, I happened to notice two blinking red lights that immediately caught my attention and piqued my curiosity. They seemed to appear at the same approximate elevation and were separated by a distance estimated to be perhaps a mile apart in an otherwise very dark area just north of and behind Brown Mountain. A considerable number of communication towers, with their blinking caution lights, dot the hilltops behind and to the south of the mountain's low crest. Even though these two lights appeared to be considerably brighter than others, I was quite confident that they were some kind of tower warning lights. Most towers, however, have a vertical array of several lights, whereas those in question were single.

The next day, I drove to Lenoir, the city located east of Brown Mountain, the lights of which are hidden from view (from the 181 Overlook) and the general location of the mysterious lights seen from the 181 Overlook. I wanted to verify that communication towers did, indeed, exist in the area north of town where the lights appeared. A cursory check revealed that there are, in fact, several of them. The next night, however, when I returned to the 181 Overlook, the two lights were gone. And during several subsequent visits over a span of three years, they never again appeared. What were they? Why did they vanish? I simply don't know. Subsequent communications with several local residents, including a pilot familiar with the area, failed to provide any insights in regard to their location or nature.

A year passed before I visited the overlook again, and, fortunately, the same spectacular panorama of glistening lights appeared over the southern half of Brown Mountain. But there was one very strange exception. High in the sky over the mountain, at an altitude estimated to be several thousand feet above local terrain, were lights identical to those of a small plane. I paid no attention to them until about ten minutes after the first sighting I noticed that, relative to nearby stars, they had not moved. In fact, the lights remained in the same position for at least an hour. A balloon would have drifted, and it is extremely doubtful that a helicopter would stay in one position for that length of time. I have no idea what it was that several of us at the site witnessed.

It was during my third visit in October of 2013 that I realized some very strange things can and do appear behind Brown Mountain. Soon after darkness fell, two very bright lights appeared in the valley to the south of the mountain. They moved slowly from left to right (east to west) and at the outset some distance from each other. Gradually, over a period of perhaps five minutes, they came together and suddenly vanished. I was sure that the lights were associated with vehicles traveling the westbound lane of I-40. A day or so later, however, I was on I-40 and realized that the dense foliage of trees bordering the highway's westbound lanes block any view of traffic from the 181 Overlook. Whatever it was that I saw had to be moving slowly *above* the treetops. The lights moved too slowly to be planes, and, unlike other aircraft (such as helicopters), no other lights were visible. Their nature and source remain a complete mystery.

The same night, another amazing and mystifying light display occurred. Above and behind the distant ridge that rims the south side of the Catawba Valley, large, slowly moving, glowing, orange-colored orbs began to appear. At first sighting, I thought they might be landing lights of several planes approaching a distant airport, their color and general appearance influenced by atmospheric conditions. But it immediately became evident that this could not be the source. They continued to appear in considerable number and move slowly in all directions before eventually vanishing behind the hills. Another possible explanation seemed to be a military exercise using flares. But the various motions of the lights seemed to rule that out. When the lights were described to several local residents, no one could explain what I had seen. Based on these personal experiences, I can attest to the fact that a considerable number of light displays seen in the vicinity of Brown Mountain continue to be a deep and intriguing mystery.

Much of the confusion existing in regard to the lights' "true" nature results from their great diversity as they appear over Brown Mountain. At dusk, or under moonlit conditions, the backdrop of terrain that rises above the ridge is clearly visible. It is on this panoramic landscape that most lights appear. Under conditions of total darkness, however, the lights seem to float in the sky above the mountain. I believe that this illusion—that the lights appear to float in space—contributes to at least some of the paranormal explanations. Appalachian State University physics and astronomy professor Daniel Caton has studied the lights for years. He believes that nearly all of them (more than 95%) are subject to simple explanation. This may be true. Based on my own experiences, however, lights do appear that remain unexplained in terms of their nature and source. And something strange has appeared during each of my visits to the site.

Most lights, including all those that I have seen, appear above or beyond Brown Mountain. I have never seen a light on the dark western side of the ridge (the side facing the 181 Overlook and Wiseman's View). Nonetheless, there are descriptions and even videos of lights on this side. These, I believe, are what the purists refer to as the "true" BMLs. Of these and other lights, there are at least a dozen theories that attempt to explain their source.[1] They range from supernatural to geological, from atmospheric to psychological, and from chemical to prosaic. Among the more bizarre theories are pranks, divine power, hunters' lanterns, and moonshine stills. Wherever a real and long-standing mystery exists, people become extremely creative as they grope for explanations of the enigmatic phenomenon. Perhaps some things are intended to remain unexplained mysteries that inspire awe and excite the imagination.

Regardless of their source or sources, the lights have appeared for a very long time. According to legend, the Cherokee and Catawba Indians first saw them as long ago as 1200 AD. Traveling the area in 1771, German engineer Gerard Will de Braham saw the lights and wrote about them. He believed that they were windborne nitrous vapors. As one would expect, through time numerous legends evolved as people attempted to explain the lights. They include the usual array of native maidens searching for lost warriors, the spirit of a slave searching for his lost master, and the restless and vengeful spirit of someone murdered long ago, among others. An entire book could be written on the light-related folklore and the various theories advanced over a span of centuries to explain them.

Ultimately, nearly every individual sees and reacts to the Brown Mountain Lights in a different way. What a person sees is based on her or his own knowledge, belief system, and perceptions. In my own experience, I have witnessed the light display in company with a large number of other viewers. Nearly everyone seems to hold his or her own interpretation of what is seen, its nature, and its source. Rarely, if ever, do observers agree on what they see or what is behind the spectacular display of lights that hover over Brown Mountain. Certainly, the beauty, mystery, and sense of awe associated with this incredible light spectacle will continue to draw thousands of viewers to Brown Mountain. And by any measure, visitors will be treated to what I believe to be one of the world's most remarkable, and in some ways most mysterious, ghost light displays.

Plumtree (Avery County):
Slippery Hill (cemetery)

Slippery Hill Cemetery is located on Squirrel Creek Road, which branches off US Highway 19E roughly halfway between Minneapolis and Plumtree. The turn-off is immediately to the south of Russell's Antiques (in 2016, the sign for the paved road was largely hidden by vegetation). Slippery Hill Cemetery begins on the left, just a short distance south of the turn-off.

The only reference I have found to the ghost light of Slippery Hill Cemetery appeared in a 1982 article in *The State* by Bertie Cantrell. Basing her information on reports from local residents, Cantrell tells a chilling tale of a light that foretells death. Strange occurrences in and around the cemetery, however, date back to at least the dawn of the twentieth century, when horsemen occasionally were startled by an "invisible presence" that jumped on their horses as they passed the cemetery.

The road passing the cemetery is steep and narrow and rounds a sharp curve just beyond the graveyard. Around the time Cantrell told her story, two young men lost their lives in separate accidents as their speeding vehicles left the road and plunged some two hundred feet into the valley of the North Toe River. According to Dixie Pittman, a local resident quoted in the article, "There have been mysterious lights seen on the graveyard by different people for many

Plumtree/Slippery Hill Cemetery

years." She and other residents evidently believed in a rather common genre of British folklore that when the light appears it always portends death. This, alone, could be reason why there seem to be no reports of a ghost light hovering over Slippery Hill Cemetery during recent years. Who, after all, wants to witness a harbinger of sure death to the viewer?

Rutherfordton (Rutherford County):
Gilboa Church (cemetery)

When traveling north on US 221 approximately three miles north of Rutherfordton, R. S. Central High School is on the left. About two-tenths of a mile beyond the school, Gilboa Church Road branches off to the right. The church is on the right (east side) in a short distance.

Two websites tell an identical tragic tale of a group of peo-

Gilboa Church and cemetery

ple leaving the Gilboa United Methodist church and being "run down" by a train. Unfortunately, the reader is left to his or her imagination in regard to when the accident supposedly occurred, how many people (if any) were killed or injured, or any other useful details. Furthermore, no legend seems to be associated with the event, which seems rather strange—if, indeed, the accident actually occurred. The two brief information sources both agree, however, that at night one can see the spirits of the deceased appearing as strange lights in the church's adjacent graveyard.

When visiting the site, I found that the "Thermal Belt Rail Trail," the old railroad right-of-way, passes between the church and cemetery. So certainly an accident such as that described above could have happened. But did it? In an attempt to dig deeper into the mystery, I was extremely fortunate to communicate with a lifelong church member and its historian, Professor David K. Yelton. About several local legends, Dr. Yelton suggests that they "were the products of bored rural teens [in the late 1940s or early 1950s] out looking to prank their friends." And in regard to the Gilboa Church lights, he notes that they "do appear in the cemetery because as one enters the [church] driveway several polished head-stones reflect the lights briefly." In regard to the supposed tragic accident, he indicated that it never happened. And as for ghosts haunting the church, Dr. Yelton noted that the house of worship was "Spirit-filled, yes . . . but not haunted by spirits."

Statesville (Iredell County):
Bostian's Bridge (railroad bridge)

Follow Buffalo Shoals Road southwest out of Statesville for one mile after it branches off Garner Bagnal Boulevard. Bostian's Bridge is on the right (west) where the railroad crosses Third Creek, just beyond a heavily excavated industrial site.

Around 2:00 a.m. on the morning of August 27, 1891, Bostian's Bridge became the site of North Carolina's most tragic railroad disaster. A passenger train traveling from Salisbury to Asheville derailed and plunged more than sixty feet into the narrow valley of Third Creek. Many passengers died from the impact or drowned in the dark swirling waters of the stream. The number of reported deaths varies from twenty-two to thirty. It seems probable that twenty-two people were killed instantly, and the higher figure includes those who died later from their injuries.

As told by Tony Reevy, a half century later, on the early morning of August 27, 1941, a woman was alone in a vehicle stranded on the road near Bostian's Bridge. Suddenly, she

Bostian's Bridge

claimed to have seen the bright lights and heard the mournful whistle of an onrushing train. As it sped across the bridge, the train suddenly derailed and crashed into the bed of Three Mile Creek—precisely as had occurred in the accident fifty years earlier. She described in some detail the twisted metal of the engine and wrecked cars and the agonizing screams and groans of the injured.

According to legend, what the unnamed woman claimed to have experienced in 1941 is repeated each year on the anniversary of the horrible train crash. (One can only wonder: Why did it take a half century for the reenactment to occur?) Various witnesses over the years say they have heard the terrible sounds of the accident and desperate cries of the injured passengers. And here the story takes yet another gruesome twist. Shortly after 2:00 a.m. on August 27, 2010—the 119th anniversary of the initial tragedy—about a dozen adventure-seeking ghost hunters were at the site hoping to witness the legendary crash. You can imagine their excitement when they saw the light of an oncoming train! Except they were *on* the bridge and the train was *real* and approaching at a speed of thirty-five to forty miles per hour. In panic, they ran in the direction of Statesville to get off the high bridge and to safety. Tragically, one young man did not make it; he was struck by the engine and killed. This serves as a sad reminder that a railroad right-of-way is private property, and those who trespass can and occasionally do place themselves in serious jeopardy. No ghost light investigation is worth losing one's life!

Statesville (Iredell County):
No known name (railroad bridge)

Old Charlotte Road becomes Amity Hill Road where it crosses Shelton Avenue on the south edge of Statesville. Follow Amity Hill Road to the crossing of Third Creek. Branch railroad passes in immediate vicinity.

Tony Reevy is the only known source of this railroad-related ghost light, which according to legend, appears only once a year. At the site located about two miles east of Bostian's Bridge, a railroad conductor supposedly fell to his death off a railroad trestle at a point where a little-used railroad crosses Third Creek. Each year, on the anniversary of his death (a date not mentioned), his ghost appears swinging a lantern. Reevy cited his source of information as a 1994 interview with Charlotte resident William Hoke. Local residents with whom I communicated were unaware of the legend.

Chapter Seven

REFLECTIONS

⚡ ⚡ ⚡

RATHER THAN "CLOSING the book," so to speak, on North Carolina's mysterious lights, I hope this volume opens new avenues of interest, exploration, and research. I have attempted to document all those lights within the state for which information was found, regardless of how scant or erroneous it may be. In some instances, I suggest the possible, if not probable, light source. However, as you now know, a small number of the state's ghost lights absolutely defy explanation based on my knowledge and that of numerous scientists and others who have studied them. Anthropologist Margaret Mead once said, "The history of scientific advancement is full of scientists investigating phenomena that the establishment did not believe were there." Unfortunately, this is not the case in regard to ghost light research and their mysterious, yet alluring, aura. It is a shame that so little serious attention has been directed—particularly by scientists—toward gaining a better understanding of these fascinating phenomena. The same holds true for the body of folktales that has evolved over time in association with the lights. I find it extremely surprising that ghost light–related legends have scarcely been touched by folklorists in North Carolina or elsewhere.

Mysterious lights appear worldwide, and they have illuminated the darkness with their eerie presence throughout recorded history. In North Carolina, reports of ghost lights place them in nearly every area of the state. And they have been reported since the dawn of European settlement (and in some instances long before, according to Native American legends). Attempts to explain their appearance and source(s) have contributed to a rich, fascinating, and varied body of folklore. One tale in particular stands out as a probable North Carolina–derived genre—the railroad accident resulting in the decapitation of a trainman whose head was never found. There are several variants of this legend, but all involve the glowing lantern held by the revenant in search of his lost head. Although similar stories do occur elsewhere (e.g., Crossett and Gurdon, Arkansas), the southeastern region of the state appears to be the source of this legend and the area in which the motif is most common. I believe that it originated with the mythical Joe Baldwin accident near present-day Maco in the late 1860s. From there, it spread throughout much of the region and beyond. As is true of many other lights, the apparently fallacious Joe Baldwin legend lives on long after the light itself vanished.

It is both disappointing and somewhat mystifying that of the fifty-four lights described in this book, only a handful still appear regularly, with another half dozen or so possibly still seen on occasion. It is possible, of course, that a number of formerly reported lights still appear, but are now ignored by observers. Two others—the Maco and Mintz Lights—did appear on a regular basis but vanished when the railroad tracks were removed over which they mysteriously hovered for more than a century. This strongly suggests the existence of some as yet unexplained relationship between steel rails and the associated display of strange lights.

I do believe that a visitor to several sites—particularly the railroad crossing on Early Station Road between Ahoskie and Aulander, the various Brown Mountain overlooks north of Morganton, or Thomas Divide Overlook on the Blue Ridge Parkway north of Cherokee—will be rewarded with an absolutely spectacular and unforgettable display of mysterious lights. What I find most interesting, and certainly something that must be considered in any attempt to explain the lights' origins, is their varied appearance. Based on my own viewing experience, the Maco Light was a basketball-sized, glowing orb that hovered at a constant height above the rails. The railroad-related lights at Early Station present an incredible display of varied colors, shapes, sizes, motions, and locations relative to the tracks. Although not associated with a railroad, the same holds true for the amazing variety of lights that I witnessed during several visits to Brown Mountain. And the bright light in the valley below Thomas Divide Overlook—that moved a considerable distance, stopped, and remained illuminated for at least an hour—was unlike any other I have seen in North Carolina or elsewhere.

In this context, it is important to recognize that many if not most lights must have at least two components—a source of energy and a means of illumination. A third factor may come into play: some catalyst that links the two (as a flashlight with batteries, a bulb, and an on-off switch). I have discussed this question with several physicists and have always come up empty-handed in terms of a plausible explanation. Evidently, many unexplained lights present a mystery that fits no currently recognized cause-effect relationship.

As mentioned in chapter 6, Charles Fort, the father of "Fortean" studies, in an attempt to explain why so many lights no longer appear, may have provided an answer in noting that "our general acceptance is that all reports upon such phenomena are colored in terms of appearances and subjects uppermost in [our] minds." That is, if we believe in and occasionally think about ghost lights, ghost lights almost certainly will appear. In this context, several things stand out. For example, the most active era of sightings seems to have been during the period immediately following World War II and before the dawn of widespread commercial television in rural North Carolina, or roughly 1945 to the early 1960s. It was a simpler time, and many folks still turned to folklore rather than science to explain unknown features or conditions. Additionally, automobiles became widely available and affordable, and gasoline was no longer rationed. The great majority of ghost light sightings and reports involved young people. Lacking many of the contemporary entertainment options, what could be more fun and exciting to do on a dark weekend night than take one's friends to a remote location to witness a spooky ghost light? This theory is supported by the fact that reports of sightings—and seemingly interest in the lights— declined sharply during and after the 1960s.

There is no doubt regarding the lure of strange, unexplained lights and their impact on the imagination. Whereas many ghost lights can be explained in simple terms—such as lights of distant vehicles—humans, by nature it seems, prefer a mystery. It is important to remember, however, that just because something is unexplained now in no way suggests that it is not subject to explanation in the future. Much of the natural world remains a mystery, so there is still a great deal left for scientists and others to discover and learn. I believe that an explanation of the source of energy for currently unexplained lights simply awaits discovery. There certainly is no need to turn to the supernatural in search of answers. Rather, we simply need more serious research directed toward the phenomenon and additional information to be gathered and analyzed.

In the final analysis, it is perhaps far more satisfying to delude ourselves and to attribute a ghost light to some mysterious paranormal source than it is to believe in a mundane common-sense explanation. Human nature, I suspect, will ensure that North Carolina's mysterious lights and luminous legends will long continue to illuminate the darkness and tantalize the curiosity of viewers.

Notes

CHAPTER 1

1. "Railghosts and Hauntings": this website lists 174 railroad-related ghost items from the United Kingdom, eight of which are similar to those occurring in North Carolina (accessed December 5, 2013).

2. A detailed definition and discussion of the various terms related to swamp gas appears in Wayland D. Hand's *Popular Beliefs and Superstitions from North Carolina.*

3. Quoted by Jennifer Osborn in Bell and Steiger, *The Source.*

CHAPTER 2

1. Guiley, *Atlas of the Mysterious in North America*; Hauck, *Haunted Places*; Kaczmarek, *Illuminating the Darkness.* Kaczmarek includes fifteen lights in North Carolina, previously the greatest number appearing in any comprehensive listing.

CHAPTER 6

1. The most comprehensive list of possible light sources of which I am aware, along with an assessment of each, appears in Kaczmarek, *Illuminating the Darkness*, pp. 81–84.

Bibliography

ACL and SAL Railroads Historical Society. n.d. "Maco N.C. What Line?" LUSENET. Accessed February 13, 2019. http://www .greenspun.com/bboard/q-and-a-fetch-msg.tcl?msg_id=002gem.

Allen, James. Personal communication (April 29, 2010).

Ball, Timothy M. October 30, 1993. "Ghostly Going-ons: Rowan County Boasts Its Share of Legends." *Salisbury Post*; p. 1.

Barnhill, Taylor. Personal communication (various, 2013).

Barry, James. 1980. *Ball Lightning and Bead Lightning.* New York: Plenum Press.

Barefoot, Daniel W. 2002. *North Carolina's Haunted Hundred,* Vol. 1, *Seaside Spectres.* Winston-Salem: John F. Blair, Publisher; pp. 61–63, 75–79.

Bell, Art, and Brad Steiger. 2002. *The Source: Journey Through the Unexplained.* New York: New American Library; p. xii.

Beitler, Stu. August 27, 1891. "Bostian's Bridge, NC Train Disaster, Aug. 1891." GenDisasters. Accessed February 13, 2019. http:// www3.gendisasters.com/north-carolina/9917/bostians-bridge -nc-train-disaster-aug-1891.

Bill, Scooter. June 1, 2009. "Teach's Light—The Ghost of Black- beard—Ocracoke Island, NC." Waymarking. Accessed February 13, 2019. http://www.waymarking.com/waymarks/WM6GM1 _Teachs_Light_The_Ghost_of_Black beard_Ocracoke_Island _NC.

Bingham, Larry. December 26, 1993. "Swamp Gas? Apparition? Lights Remain a Mystery." *Durham Herald-Sun;* pp. G1 & G5.

boakley99. September 26, 2012. "The Screaming Bridge." Your- GhostStories. Accessed February 13, 2019. http://www.your ghoststories.com/real-ghost-story.php?story=16538.

Black, Harold. February 5, 1961. "A New Ghost Light in North Carolina." *Raleigh News & Observer*; p. III–3.

Bord, Janet, and Colin Bord. 1989. *Unexplained Mysteries of the 20th Century.* Chicago: Contemporary Books; p. 138.

Botkin, Ben, and Alvin Harlow. 1953. *A Treasure of Railroad Folklore.* New York: Crown Publishers; pp. 398–399.

Booker, W. H. April 11, 1965. "Death Followed Light's Appearances." in *Raleigh News & Observer*; p. III–2.

Brantley, Michael. Personal communication (2016).

Brooker, Louise Robertson. 1971. *Ghosts and Witches of Martin County.* Williamston, NC: Enterprise Publishing Company; pp. 25–27.

Burke, James C. 2012. *James C. Burke Papers, Vol. 1: The Joe Baldwin File.* Ebook. https://archive.org/details/JamesC.BurkePapersvol .1-TheJoeBaldwinFile.

"Burke County's Mysterious Light Still Baffles Investigators." *Charlotte Observer*, September 23, 1913; p. 2.

Byers, Thomas. June 10, 2013. "True North Carolina Ghost Stories." HubPages. Accessed February 13, 2019. http://crazyhorsesghost .hubpages.com/hub/True-North-Carolina-Ghost-Stories-2.

Cantrell, Bertie. April 1982. "The Legend of Slippery Hill." *The State*, 49:1; pp. 17, 31.

Carden, Gary, and Nina Anderson. 1994. *Belled Buzzards, Hucksters & Grieving Specters: Appalachian Tales, Strange, True and Legendary.* Asheboro, NC: Down Home Press.

Carter, Catherine T. 1992. *Ghost Tales of the Moratoc.* Winston-Salem: John F. Blair, Publisher; pp. 58–64, 136–142.

Casstevens, Frances H. 2009. "Mysterious Lights," in *Ghosts of the North Carolina Piedmont.* Charleston, SC: Haunted America; p. 71

Camo4x4s. "North Carolina Ghost Light Legend Caught on Film!!!" YouTube video, 6:49. December 19, 2006. http://www.youtube .com/watch?v=bMkzoI4241Y&feature=player_embedded#.

chavdawg. "The Bowie Light." YouTube Video, 4:04. November 12, 2008. http://www.youtube.com/watch?v=gVdczEkDOzc.

Clayton, Norma. Personal communication (various, 2016).

Coit, John. December 7, 1969. "Strange Light in a Dark Swamp."
  Raleigh News & Observer; p. V-1.

Concord Standard Weekly. December 14, 1888.

Concord Times. December 14, 1888.

Corliss, William R. 2001. *Remarkable Luminous Phenomena in Na-
  ture* (references to marine related lights; pp. 331–384.) and (1977)
  Handbook of Unusual Natural Phenomena (Chapter 1, "Luminous
  Phenomena"; pp. 1–86). Glen Arm, MD: Sourcebook Project.

Eckard, J. Eric. October 30, 2005. "Ghost Stories Haunt Twin Counties." *Rocky Mount Telegram;* pp. 1–2.

Edwards, Daniel T. "The Haunted Light at Clarkton." Accessed
  April 27, 2012. http://www.wirenot.net/X/Stories/Ghost_2
  /Ghost_H-I/haunted_light_at_clarkton.shtml (site discontinued).

Edwards, Stuart M. Personal communication (June 2013).

Fleming, Jason. "Thomas Divide Lights 2011." Vimeo video, 8:56.
  2012. http://vimeo.com/27979481.

Fort, Charles. 1923/1974. *The Complete Books of Charles Fort (New
  Lands).* New York: Dover Publications; pp. 417–422, 457–460.

Frizzell, Michael A. January/February 1984. "Investigating the
  Brown Mountain Lights." *INFO Journal,* 9:22.

"Ghostly American Legends." *Life* 43(18), October 28, 1957;
  pp. 88–89.

Ghosts of America. Accessed February 13, 2019. http://www.ghosts
  ofamerica.com.

greattenchim. July 19, 2005. "The Maco Railroad Light." Ghost Vil-
  lage. Accessed February 13, 2019. http://www.ghostvillage.com
  /ghostcommunity/index.php?s=1cfc44d124db52cecd76deb
  1459c1ede&showtopic=9278&st=0&p=193419&#entry193419.

Green, Ann. October 31, 1991. "The Phantom Train of Catsburg."
  Durham Herald-Sun; pp. A8–9.

Green River Preserve. Accessed February 13, 2019. http://www
  .greenriverpreserve.org/.

Gritzner, Charles F. January–February 2002. "What Is Where,

Why There, and Why Care?" *Journal of Geography*, 101(1); pp. 38–40.

Guiley, Rosemary Ellen. 1995. *Atlas of the Mysterious in North America*. New York: Facts on File.

Hairr, John. 1995. *Bizarre Tales of Cape Fear Country*. Fuquay-Varina, NC: Triangle Books; pp. 60–63.

Hall, Gary. 1973. "The Big Tunnel." *Indiana Folklore*, 1(2); pp. 139–173. Also in Linda Degh (ed.). 1980. *Indiana Folklore: A Reader*. Bloomington: Indiana University Press; pp. 225–257.

Hand, Wayland D., ed. 1964. "Jack-O'-Lanterns," in *Popular Beliefs and Superstitions from North Carolina*. Durham: Duke University Press; pp. 148–150.

Hannah, Mike. August 31, 1988. "Mystery Light Show." *Watauga Democrat*, Boone, NC; pp. 1–14.

Harden, John. 1954. *Tar Heel Ghosts*. Chapel Hill: University of North Carolina Press; pp. 44–51, 170.

Harden, John. 1949. "The Brown Mountain Lights" in *The Devil's Tramping Ground*. Chapel Hill: University of North Carolina Press; pp. 127–137.

Hauck, Dennis William. 2002. *Haunted Places: The National Directory*. New York: Penguin Books; pp. 317, 320.

"Haunted Coastal North Carolina." City-Data. Last modified October 10, 2014. http://www.city-data.com/forum/coastal-north -carolina/176934-haunted-coastal-north-carolina.html#ixzz2 b7Lr6j55.

Hester, Margaret. November 10, 2006. "The Thomas Divide." Western Carolinian. Accessed February 13, 2019. http://www.western carolinian.com/mobile/2.2006/the-thomas-divide-1.145891.

Hodges, Sarah. Fall, 2009. "The Screaming Bridge." *North Carolina's Eastern Living Magazine* 1(1); pp. 11–12.

Holzer, Hans. 1972. *The Phantoms of Dixie*. Indianapolis: The Bobbs-Merrill Company; pp. 68–90.

Johnson, F. Roy. 1962. *Legends and Myths of North Carolina's*

Roanoke-Chowan Area. Murfreesboro, TN: Johnson Publishing Company; pp. 44, 74–76.

Kaczmarek, Dale. 2003. *Illuminating the Darkness: The Mystery of Spook Lights.* Alton, IL: Whitechapel Productions Press.

Kasper, Andrew. January 23, 2013. "Theories Swirl around Perplexing Mountain Lights." *Smoky Mountain News* (Waynesville, NC).

Lancaster, Lindsay. June 5, 2007. "Tiny Blue Ghost Fireflies Make Their Annual Appearance." *Hendersonville (NC) Times-News.*

Little, Dr. Greg. July 2003. "The Brown Mountain, NC, Lights Videotaped: A Field Observation—July 2003." *Alternate Perceptions Magazine*; p. 7.

lunanightmyst. "aulander, nc ghost light on the tracks." YouTube Video, 10:51. April 29, 2010. https://www.youtube.com/watch?v=13G2OZdJ7gc

Manley, Roger. 2007. *Weird Carolinas.* New York: Sterling Publishing; pp. 8, 173–174.

McDowell, Silas. n.d. "A Spectre Cavalry Fight at Chimney Rock Pass, Blue Ridge, N.C.," in the McDowell Papers at the University of North Carolina, Chapel Hill; 13 pages.

Montell, William Lynwood. 2010. *Tales of Kentucky Ghosts.* Lexington: University of Kentucky Press; pp. 150–151.

Mooney, James. 1992. *History, Myths and Sacred Formulas of the Cherokee.* Asheville, NC: Bright Mountain Books.

Moore, Aaron. Personal communication (September 1, 2013).

"Morpheus Bridge." Real Haunts. Accessed February 13, 2019. http://www.realhaunts.com/united-states/morpheus-bridge/.

NC Ghost Guide. Accessed February 13, 2019. http://www.ncghostguide.byethost12.com/index.html.

Neal, Jerry. April 5, 2002. "Wehahutta Lights." True Ghosts Stories Archive. Accessed February 13, 2019. http://www.ghosts.org/ghostlights/wehahuttalights.html.

Newton, Rev. George. September 15, 1806. "Extraordinary Phenomenon." *Raleigh Register and State Gazette.*

Nickell, Joe. January/February 2016. "The Brown Mountain Lights: Solved! (Again!). *Skeptical Inquirer,* 40:1; pp. 24–27.

norman. November 11, 2011. "Train Brakeman Still Looking." YourGhostStories. Accessed February 13, 2019. http://www .yourghoststories.com/real-ghost-story.php?story=4557.

Obiwan. January 29, 2019. "Maco Light." True Ghosts Stories Archive. Accessed February 13, 2019. http://ghosts.org/maco-light/.

Odenwalk, Sten, ed. 2001. "Brown Mountain Lights, North Carolina." AstronomyCafe. Accessed February 13, 2019. http://www .astronomycafe.net/weird/lights/brown1.htm.

paranormalresearchersofecass. February 17, 2012. "Final Case Report for Investigation #3." P.R.E.C.A. Accessed February 13, 2019. http://preca.webs.com/apps/blog/show/12467976-final-case -report-for-investigation-3.

Parris, John A., Jr. December 1936. "Superstitions of the Indians." *The State,* 4(27); pp. 5, 18.

"Railghosts and Hauntings." ParanormalDatabase. Accessed December 5, 2013, and February 13, 2019. http://www.paranormaldata base.com/reports/rail.php?pageNum_paradata=1&totalRows _paradata=174

Reevy, Tony. 1998. *Ghost Train! American Railroad Ghost Legends.* Marceline, MO: Walsworth Publishing Company.

Renegar, Michael F. 2005. "Phantom Headlights," in *Roadside Revenants: And Other North Carolina Ghosts and Legends.* Fairview, NC: Bright Mountain Books; pp. 10–13

Rivers, Michael. 2010. *Ghosts of the North Carolina Shores.* Atglen, PA: Schiffer Publishing; pp. 53–55.

Roberts, Bruce, and Nancy Roberts. 1970. *This Haunted Land.* Charlotte, NC: McNally and Loftin, Publishers; pp. 9–13.

Roberts, Nancy. 1959/1985. *Illustrated Guide to Ghosts & Mysterious Occurrences in the Old North State.* Asheville, NC: Bright Mountain Books; pp. 28–31.

Roberts, Nancy. 1991. *North Carolina Ghosts & Legends.* Columbia: University of South Carolina Press; pp. 97–100.

Roberts, Nancy. 1993. *Ghosts of the Southern Mountains & Appalachia*. Columbia, SC: University of South Carolina Press; pp. 120–124.

Rollins, Terry. n.d. "The Light at Maco Station." ibiblio. Accessed February 13, 2019. http://www.ibiblio.org/ghosts/maco3.html.

Russell, Randy, and Janet Barnett. 1988. *Mountain Ghost Stories and True Tales of Western North Carolina*. Winston-Salem, NC: John F. Blair, Publisher.

Pressley, J. M. 2013. *Ghost Lights of North Carolina: Eerie Sightings in the Tar Heel State.*

Sagan, Carl. 1995. *The Demon Haunted World*. New York: Random House; p. 15.

Schenck, Sandy. Personal communication (2012).

Second Annual Catalogue of the East Carolina Teacher's Training School. 1911. Greenville, NC: The Reflector Co., Printers.

Schlosser, S. E. n.d. "Blackbeard's Ghost." American Folklore. Last modified June 10, 2017. http://americanfolklore.net/folklore/2010/07/blackbeards_ghost.html.

Schlosser, S. E. n.d. "Maco Ghost Light." American Folklore. Last modified June 10, 2017. http://americanfolklore.net/folklore/2009/03/the_maco_ghost_light.html.

Schlosser, S. E. n.d. "Phantom Train Wreck." American Folklore. Last modified June 10, 2017. http://americanfolklore.net/folklore/2010/07/the_phantom_train_wreck.html.

"Screaming Bridge." May 6, 2014. Hauntings. Accessed February 13, 2019. http://hauntin.gs/listing/screaming-bridge-4/.

Skew Arkians (Junior Historical Club). 1980. "Legend of Swinson's Light," in *Weird Tales of Martin County*. Williamston, NC: Junior Historical Club, Bear Grass School (Elizabeth Robertson, Advisor); pp. 7–8.

Sparks, Nicholas. 2005. *True Believer*. New York: Warner Books.

Steelman, Ben. July 18, 2013. "Did Grover Cleveland Ever See the Maco Light?" *Wilmington* (NC) *StarNews*. Accessed February 13, 2019. http://www.myreporter.com/2013/07/did-grover-cleveland-ever-see-the-maco-light/.

Steelman, Ben. March 18, 2009. "What Is the Maco Light?" *StarNews*. Accessed February 13, 2019. http://www.myreporter .com/2009/03/the-maco-light/.

Steelman, Ben. October 8, 2008. "The Maco Light: Brunswick's 'True' Ghost Story." *StarNews*. Accessed February 13, 2019. http://www.starnewsonline.com/article/20081010/ARTICLES /810100258?p=7&tc=pg.

Taylor, Troy. 1998. "The Ghosts of Smithfield." Ghosts of the Prairie. Accessed February 13, 2019. http://www.prairieghosts.com /smithfield.html.

Taylor, Troy. 1998. "The Maco Railroad Light." Ghosts of the Prairie. Accessed February 13, 2019. http://www.prairieghosts.com /maco.html.

"The Chimney Rock Apparitions." North Carolina Ghosts. Accessed February 13, 2019. http://www.northcarolinaghosts.com /mountains/chimney-rock-apparitions.php.

"The Maco Light." North Carolina Ghosts. Accessed February 13, 2019. http://www.northcarolinaghosts.com/coast/macolight .php.

The Shadowlands. 1994. Last modified 2017. http://www.theshadow lands.net

They, Edrick. 2005. *Ghost Stories of North Carolina*. Vancouver, BC: Lone Pine Publishing.

Thomas, Heath. April 11, 1965. "Strange Lights Still Seen in Rowan." *Raleigh News & Observer*; p. III–2.

Walser, Richard. 1980. *North Carolina Legends*. Raleigh: North Carolina Division of Archives and History; pp. 50–52.

Warren, Joshua P. November 11, 2004. "Report on the Cause of the Mysterious Brown Mountain Lights." Asheville, NC: L.E.M.U.R.; p. 8.

Warren, Joshua P. 2013. *Brown Mountain Lights: A Viewing Guide*. Ebook. http://shadowboxent.brinkster.net/bml%20viewing%20 guide_9-16-13.pdf.

Whedbee, Charles H. 1966. *Legends of the Outer Banks and Tarheel Tidewater.* Winston-Salem, NC: John F. Blair, Publisher.

Wigginton, Eliot, ed. 1973. *Foxfire 2.* New York: Anchor Books; pp. 346–347.

Zepke, Terrance. 2001. "The Inexplicable Vander Light," in *The Best Ghost Tales of North Carolina.* Sarasota, FL: Pineapple Press; pp. 29–30.

Zepke, Terrance. 2005. "The Mysterious Pactolus Light," in *Ghosts and Legends of the Carolina Coasts.* Sarasota, FL: Pineapple Press; pp. 144–147.

Zepke, Terrance. 2006. *The Best Ghost Tales of North Carolina,* 2nd ed. Sarasota, FL: Pineapple Press; pp. 18–23, 127–128.

Acknowledgments

Hundreds of people contributed information that in some way made this book possible. My deepest thanks to you all. Without your interest and kind assistance, this study could not have come to fruition.

A substantial number of individuals provided particularly valuable information on one or more lights, or some other aspect of the study. In alphabetical order and without reference to professional titles, they include James Allen, Melanie Armstrong, Jay Barnes, Taylor Barnhill, Karen Boyer, Norma Clayton, Ted Coyle, Stewart Edwards, George Frizzell, and Tim Hall. Others who assisted are Roger Kammerer, Kerry McDuffie, Joy Salyers, Patricia Sawin, Sandy Scheck, Bland Simpson, Elizabeth Sparrow, Dirck Spencer, Traci Thompson, Jonathan Underwood, Mike Wilkins, and David Yelton. Your contributions are greatly appreciated.

My thanks to Janet Gritzner and Bill Nelson for their preparation of the maps and to Carol Young for her meticulous editing of the initial manuscript. She taught me more about passive voice than I ever wanted to know!

I am deeply indebted to the professional team at Blair, with whom it was a real pleasure to work: Lynn York, publisher; Robin Miura, senior editor and associate publisher; Danielle Dyal, copy editor; Arielle Hebert, operations director; and Carla Avilés-Jimenez, marketing assistant.

In a study of this nature, it is important to recognize the role of those hundreds of people who, over a span of centuries, "saw the lights" and through legend kept them illuminated.

Finally, to my wife, Yvonne, thank you for your enthusiastic support of this project and for keeping the home fires burning and our two dogs, Punkin and Jada, cared for during my numerous trips to North Carolina to conduct field and library research for this book.